# *Beyond* BURLAP

Idaho's Famous Potato™ Recipes
*Junior League of Boise*

First Edition
First Printing, September 1997
20,000
Copyright© 1997 The Junior League of Boise, Inc.
5266 Franklin Road, Boise, Idaho 83705

This book is a collection of our favorite potato recipes, which are not necessarily original recipes.
For additional copies, use the order blank in the back of the book or direct inquiries to:

### *The Junior League of Boise*

*5266 Franklin Road, Boise, ID 83705*
*1-888-340-5754*
*(208) 342-8851*
Library of Congress Catalog number: 97-72093
ISBN: 0-913743-97-6

Designed, manufactured, and edited in the United States of America by
Favorite Recipes® Press
an imprint of

**FRP**

2451 Atrium Way, Nashville, Tennessee 37214
1-800-358-0560

Cover Photography: Roasted Potatoes and Red Bell Pepper with Sage and Garlic
Cover Food Photography by Stan Sinclair, Food Styling by Rebecca Robison
Illustrations by Margaret Hepworth

"Idaho Potatoes®," "Grown in Idaho®," and "Famous Potatoes™" are trademarks of the
Idaho Potato Commission and are used with permission of the Idaho Potato Commission.

*Proceeds from the sale of* Beyond Burlap . . . Idaho's Famous Potato Recipes *will benefit the
community and the charitable works of The Junior League of Boise, Inc.*

# THE JUNIOR LEAGUE OF BOISE, INC.

*The Junior League of Boise is an organization of women
committed to promoting voluntarism,
developing the potential of women, and to improving the community
through the effective action and leadership of trained volunteers.
Its purpose is exclusively educational and charitable.*

— *Mission*

Since its founding in 1928, The Junior League of Boise has originated more
than 200 community projects and programs. Many of these still continue to benefit
our community today. This list is a brief sampling of our good works.

Childcare Center for the Homeless at Community House

Learning Lab Computerized Teaching Center for Reading and Writing

Renaissance Faire Period Event for Families

School Age Child Care providing Before and After School Children's Programs

Discovery Center of Idaho Hands-On Science Museum

Ronald McDonald House Lodging for Families of Cancer Patients

PAYADA Parents and Youth Against Drug Abuse

Guardian Ad Litem Court-Appointed Child Advocacy System

Bound to Please Cookbook

Second Time Around Thrift Shop

Boise School Volunteers

Children's Zoo

# EDITORIAL TEAM

*Editors-in-Chief*
Suzanne Groff Lierz     LeAnn Blanksma South

*Food and Recipe Editor*
Lauri Burgener

*Associate Food Editors*
Cheryl Bruehl     Patty O'Neill     Mary Ann Roberts     Nancy Thompson

*Copy Editor*
Kathleen Marion Carr

*Art Director*
Andrea Thornton-Rothstein

*Art Production Associates*
Kathlyn Johans     Katherine Kirk

*Marketing Editor*
Ronda Wiltse

*Associate Marketing Editors*
Amy Blickenstaff     Dana Cocales     Kari Guymon
Nikki Meek     Lynn Rubel     Terri Schultz

*Distribution Manager*
Loretta Madison

*Financial Business Manager*
Teresa Lyon

*Advisors*
Linda Gossett     Romaine Galey Hon     Virginia Pellegrini

*Editorial Consultant*
Romaine Galey Hon

# Table of CONTENTS

# BEYOND BURLAP

*is dedicated to the*
*people of Idaho…*
*who made the potato famous.*

The name *Beyond Burlap* comes from the burlap bags

that potatoes were packed in for many, many years.

We find the most common thread (burlap thread, that is)

to identify Idaho's potato and its potato history is the burlap bag.

We think the cookbook's name is a way to give you the

best potato recipes that are *beyond* the ordinary.

All these favorite recipes are kitchen-tested and come with

the seal of approval from some of the best cooks in Idaho,

members of the Junior League of Boise, and friends.

# BEYOND BURLAP: PICKING POTATOES, PEOPLE, AND PLACES

This cookbook is for people who love potatoes. Nothing could be better than having the best potato recipes at your fingertips with *Beyond Burlap*. This cookbook features the russet potato that made Idaho famous, but you will see that it's not the only potato featured. Here are almost 200 kitchen-tested potato recipes using a variety of potatoes.

We think the recipes in *Beyond Burlap* are the best potato recipes ever found in one place. (After sampling these recipes, we believe that you will agree.) There are old favorites with hints to help you bake, scallop, or mash a better potato. You also will find many of our favorite potato recipes collected from friends, neighbors, and relatives who keep cooking those beloved hand-me-downs. We include favorite potato recipes from some of Idaho's best chefs. After much evaluating, only potato recipes withstanding the scrutiny of our testers are found in *Beyond Burlap*.

We kept *Beyond Burlap* simple and easy to use, but still a cookbook that will appeal to all potato fans, whether experienced cooks or not. Some days you have less time to prepare that "potato" than others, so we included quick-and-easy potato recipes. If watching your weight is a concern, there are potatoes for you, the calorie-conscious cook. Vegetarians will find a wide variety to suit their needs. Many of the recipes are aimed toward families who gather for good food and good conversation. Finally, finish your meals off with some of the best desserts imaginable— made with potatoes.

We hope that this cookbook will prompt your curiosity about Idaho, its people and places, and, of course, its famous potato—the Burbank Russet. An extra bonus with *Beyond Burlap* is that it introduces some of the wonderful places in Idaho. Highlighting just a few of our well-known locations, we show you a bit beyond the potato. We invite you to find out more about our state. In the back of the book, you will find sources for more information. We also have included some stories from Idaho authors about living in Idaho. Their stories will make you laugh as you experience the fun of our "famous potato" state.

Thank you for buying this book. Your purchase of *Beyond Burlap* makes the Junior League of Boise community projects possible.

# HISTORICAL BACKGROUND OF THE COMMON POTATO

The Peruvian Incas were the first people known to have included the potato in their diets and culture—around 3000 B.C. After conquering the Incas, the Spaniards probably took the potato to Europe early in the sixteenth century. The Spaniards adopted the Peruvian name for the common potato ("papa"); this possibly was later combined with the West Indian name for sweet potato ("batata") to become the English-version "potato."

The potato was met with much superstition when it was first introduced in Europe. It seemed very similar to a poisonous plant species known as nightshade. To make matters worse for the vegetable, it was never mentioned in the Bible. But this did not deter most of the European noble and ruling classes, who included it in their meals as a delicacy. When the potato was found to be a productive crop, easily providing five times as much food as grains, it spread throughout the world as a year-round food source to feed the masses.

No one is absolutely certain how the potato came to the United States.

One account has the English introducing the crop to Colonial America. As this version goes, Sir Walter Raleigh's cousin, Sir Richard Grenville, and one of Raleigh's men, Sir Francis Drake, sailed in 1538 to fight the Spaniards in the Caribbean. Grenville, on his way to do battle, carried a group of colonists to Roanoke, Virginia. Then Drake allegedly agreed to restock the colonists' supplies upon his return from the Caribbean. Historians believe that it may have been Drake who stopped in Cartagena, Colombia, and bought or traded for the potatoes that later were left in Virginia.

The first record of the vegetable in America is in "Watson's Annals of Philadelphia." The author said that common sentiment at the time of the potato's introduction was that "it would shorten men's lives and make them unhealthy. . . ." As luck would have it, this was proven untrue. The potato began to thrive in America.

Historically, the common potato's best-known contribution to America resulted from the devastation caused by the Great Potato Famine in Ireland in 1845 and 1846. The potato, at the time, was the primary food source of the Irish and was the main feed for their

farm animals. A fungus developed and spread throughout the country's primary food source, wiping it out. The famine caused more than a million fatalities and the great exodus of the Irish to America.

## THE IDAHO POTATO

Henry Harmon Spalding, a Presbyterian missionary, grew the first potato in what was to become Idaho Territory. An astute man, Spalding built a mission in 1836 in Lapwai to minister to the souls of the Nez Perce Indians and to change the Indians' lifestyle.

Spalding's intent was to show the Nez Perce that an agrarian existence could provide them a new way of life. No longer would they need to depend on the rapidly dwindling buffalo population. By 1838, Spalding had seventy to eighty Nez Perce families farming; some of these families grew one hundred bushels of potatoes. It is said that those Nez Perce Indians were the first to sell or barter potatoes to pioneer settlers passing through the territory.

The first permanent white settlers in Idaho were farmers sent by the Church of Jesus Christ of Latter-Day Saints to colonize a location north of the Salt Lake Valley. These Mormon colonists, believing they were still in Utah, selected a site just across the state line in what is now Idaho. Potatoes were one of the first items planted. In the summer of 1860, these farmers raised thirty-three bushels of potatoes. Then, these and other early potato farmers began to supply potatoes as a food source for the men in the lead and silver mining camps. However, it was not until the Idaho gold rush that the Idaho potato farmers began to prosper.

Most of the potatoes grown in Idaho today are Russet Burbank. The Russet Burbank seen in supermarkets can be attributed to two men, Luther Burbank and Lon D. Sweet. In 1872, Burbank was able to plant and cultivate in his New England garden twenty-three seedlings derived from an Early Rose potato variety. The seeds grew and produced tubers. Burbank found some tubers hardier, with two to three times more potato output than other varieties. He tenderly cultivated these tubers into a potato he named the Burbank.

The Russet Burbank or Idaho potato was developed by Sweet, who was able to grow a slightly different variation of the Burbank potato, but with an added value: It was resistant to blight. Thus, the Idaho potato looks a lot like a Burbank potato, but has a rougher, or netted, skin.

It is commonly said that it is not the Russet Burbank that made Idaho famous, but rather Idaho that made the Russet Burbank famous. The combination of Idaho's warm days and cool nights, its mineral-rich volcanic soil, and the farmers' controlled watering through irrigation has made ideal growing conditions and ideal potatoes.

Among the many people who were central to the success of the Idaho potato, two are legendary: Joe Marshall and J. R. Simplot.

Marshall identified strongly with the Idaho potato and had a strong desire to make it the best product possible. Marshall was able to convince Union Pacific Railroad to provide more rail cars, enabling the Idaho potato to be marketed in the Midwest and in eastern cities. He promoted the best quality seed available, thereby establishing a seed industry worthy of today's world-famous Idaho potato.

All who knew Marshall would agree that he never compromised when it came to his high-quality standards for the potato. He required employees to replace bruised or damaged potatoes that were accidentally dropped so that his customers would never receive a bad Idaho potato. This quality control paid off. One of the better restaurants in Chicago bought a shipment of Marshall's exceptional and large potatoes. The Chicago restaurant featured the "big" potatoes in its restaurant window, and the clientele were overwhelmed. It was this kind of marketing that launched the Idaho potato as a star.

Simplot also identified strongly with the potato and had a need to strive for innovations in its use. In his early years, Simplot was the one who developed dehydrated potatoes and sold them to the government for the G.I.s in World War II. And it was an employee of Simplot's, Ray Dunlap, who invented the frozen French fry by freezing, thawing, and frying—now known as reconstituting. Simplot's companies now supply McDonald's with more than 50 percent of their frozen French fries. In addition, Simplot's companies now use a billion pounds of potatoes a year for Simplot's innovations.

Today, the Idaho potato industry contributes $2.6 billion to Idaho's economy. Fifty-eight percent of all Idaho potatoes are used to make process products such as frozen, dehydrated, or canned potatoes. Twenty-six percent of the Idaho potato crop is shipped fresh, ten percent is certified for seed, and the rest of the crop is unusable. The potato is the most important vegetable crop in the world and the third-most-important food crop. Production is projected to increase as more and more people of the world come to enjoy and depend upon the potato.

## NUTRITIONAL AND HEALTH ASPECTS OF POTATOES

An eight-ounce potato is not the fattening vegetable that past conventional wisdom thought. A potato, baked, boiled, or steamed, without butter, has only 145 calories. It is what we put on (or cook with) the potato that causes the calories to mount.

However the potato is prepared, it is a nutritious addition to a meal. Potatoes are one of the best sources of dietary fiber. They are high in vitamin C, iron, thiamine, niacin, and riboflavin.

To maintain the maximum amount of these nutrients in your prepared potato, cook the potato with its skin intact or lightly peeled, because these nutrients are stored right below the skin's surface. And, if you boil your potato, you might consider reusing the liquid as needed for mashing to assure no loss of these healthy nutrients. Another interesting health attribute of the potato is its potassium content. Medical research has shown that the potato, if baked or steamed, has the kind of potassium that lowers cholesterol and contributes to an individual's healthy potassium level. The potato's potassium (more than in a single banana) counteracts the body's salt intake. This reduces the risk of strokes, high blood pressure, and heart disease.

## POPULAR VARIETIES OF POTATOES

*Russet Burbank:* Best known as the Idaho potato and the baking potato. A large oval potato with brown skin and white flaky flesh, it is ideal for baking, mashing, deep-frying, or including as an ingredient in a recipe. The Russet Arcadia is grown in Maine and other states and is similar in appearance to the Russet Burbank. (The Russet Burbank is recommended as the most versatile and best all-purpose choice, and, by a landslide, the best "baked" potato.)

*White Potato or Eastern Potato:* May be known as the Superior, Kennebec, Katahdin, Maine, Delaware, Long Island, or Canada. A medium-size round potato with a light tan color inside. When cooked, its texture has a finer consistency than yellow potatoes. The White Potato is also recommended as a fine all-purpose choice.

*Large or Baby Yukon Gold:* Yellow potatoes with a thin yellow skin, a round shape, and a light tan color inside. Baby Yukon Gold is recommended for roasting, steaming, boiling, or barbecuing.

*Small red or new potatoes:* Round, crisp, white-fleshed potato. Recommended for roasting, steaming, or barbecuing.

*Red Pontiac:* White flesh, round shape, red color. Recommended for roasting or pan frying.

*Sweet Potatoes or Yams:* Unrelated to the potato except in form. Light to deep-red skin and yellow to orange flesh that is sweet when cooked.

## BUYING AND STORING POTATOES

Select potatoes that are well-formed, smooth, and firm with few eyes, and that have no discoloration, cracks, bruises, or soft spots. Avoid green potatoes; they have been overexposed to light and will have a bitter taste. It is also a good idea to select potatoes of about the same size so they will cook at the same rate.

Do not wash potatoes before storing them; washing causes the potatoes to decay. Unwashed potatoes can be stored in a dry, well-ventilated, dark place for up to three months if the temperature is between forty-five and fifty degrees Fahrenheit. Never store potatoes in the refrigerator; the cold will cause the potato starch to turn to sugar, making the potato too sweet. If you must store your potatoes at a higher temperature than forty-five to fifty degrees, buy only a week's worth of potatoes at a time. This way, the potato always will maintain its good flavor and its nutritional value.

### How to Cook Potatoes
Scrub each potato clean by rubbing the potato with a sponge or vegetable brush. Pat dry.

### Baking Potatoes
The best way to bake a potato is to put it in a 425-degree oven directly on the rack and bake for 45 to 60 minutes, depending on the size of the potato. Do not wrap that Idaho potato in aluminum foil when baking! The foil holds in moisture and steams the potato, resulting in a boiled texture. Remember to turn the potato halfway through the baking time so you will brown both sides of it. The potato is baked when it responds to a squeeze—but don't forget to use an oven mitt. Do not overbake a potato, or the skin will tend to dry or shrivel. If you are not serving the potato immediately, wrap it in aluminum foil after it is baked to prevent the skin from shriveling. Never use a knife to open a baked potato. It will flatten the surface and alter the normal fluffy texture. Instead, "blossom" the potato by making an "X" on the top of the potato with the tines of a fork. Gently squeeze the potato from both ends and fluff the pulp.

### Barbecuing Potatoes
If you are going to barbecue the potatoes on skewers, make sure you heat the skewers first. This will prevent the center of the potato from turning brown.

### Microwaving Potatoes
If microwaving, prick the potatoes with a fork and wrap in a paper towel. Place the potatoes about an inch apart and cook on high about four to five minutes per potato (four medium potatoes are cooked after sixteen to twenty minutes, depending upon your microwave's wattage); turn the potatoes halfway through the baking time. Remember, microwaved potatoes will continue to cook after baking, so do not overcook them.

### Boiling Potatoes
It is suggested that you not peel a potato before cooking it. The potato's skin preserves the nutrients and the most flavor while the potato is being boiled. Remove the skin after the potato is cooked and has cooled enough to handle. If you choose to peel your potato before boiling, then do so right before cooking. (To avoid discoloration of a peeled potato, add salt or lemon juice to your cooking water.)

### Mashing Potatoes
After boiling potatoes (see boiled potato directions), drain the liquid and reserve. Mash the hot potatoes either by hand or with your mixer. Add $1/4$ cup butter (margarine) and $1/2$ cup of liquid for every four potatoes. Use reserved potato liquid, hot milk, sour cream, or broth. Mash until smooth. If you like country-style mashed potatoes, leave the skins intact before mashing.

# *Appetizers*

## *I*S IDAHO IOWA?

Most of us didn't think it was possible, but the National Governors' Conference has produced something of interest to Idahoans.

 Because most people don't lie awake nights worrying about Canadian trade barriers, the Fair Labor Standards Act, or most of the other items on the governors' agenda, I decided to use the conference to shed some light on one of Idaho's most serious and longest running problems, namely Iowa.

Think about it. How many times have you heard the words "Boise, Iowa" on national television? How many times have you been subject to cutting remarks about being from a state that is criminally flat? How many eastern friends do you have who are convinced that you live in the hogbelt?

Even governors think Idaho is Iowa. Last week, when a local reporter called the offices of most of the nation's governors to see how many planned to attend the conference, she got an answer she wasn't expecting: "Sure we'll be there," one of the governors replied. "We're looking forward to coming out there to Iowa."

The reporter didn't remember which state that particular governor represented. My guess is Utah.

Like most Idahoans, I am accustomed to being mistaken for an Iowan. (All true Idahoans accept this as an inexorable fact of life.) One thing I've always wondered, though, is whether it works both ways.

Do people in Iowa have to put up with being mistaken for Idahoans? Do they get mail addressed to Des Moines, Idaho? Do New Yorkers marveling at Iowa's tall corn shake their heads and say they didn't know potatoes grew on trees?

To learn the answers, I spoke with Iowa Governor Terry Branstad.

"Yes, it's a problem in Iowa, too," he said. "It happens all the time. People are always saying, 'how's the potato crop coming along out there?'"

The confusion between the states, he said, inspired the University of Iowa to print a T-shirt with its name in large letters and, underneath in smaller letters, the words, "Idaho City, Ohio."

Are there physical similarities, previously overlooked geographical likenesses that might explain the confusion?

"Well, Iowa isn't as flat as people think," Branstad replied, "but Idaho is definitely steeper. We used to think the highest point in Iowa was a glacial moraine. Then we thought it was the Ocheyedan Mound, and then somebody proved that it was actually some farmer's hog lot."

In one way, Iowans have it worse than Idahoans.

"It's more common for us to be confused with Idaho," Branstad said, "but people also get us mixed up with Ohio. The classic example was President Ford standing right under a sign that said 'Iowa State University' and saying how nice it was to be in Ohio."

Iowa and Idaho, the governor added, have more in common than just being confused with each other. Fourteen former governors of Idaho, he said, were natives of Iowa.

"Also Iowans are known for being friendly, and of all the governors' conventions I've attended, the people in Idaho are the friendliest. The problem isn't with Iowa or Idaho. It's the other forty-eight states that need to learn the difference. Especially those easterners."

— *by Tim Woodward*

 ## FETA SHRIMP TRIANGLES

*Yield: 10 servings*

5 pita pocket breads
$1/2$ cup unsalted butter, softened
1 small russet potato, shredded
    (about $1/2$ cup), or $1/2$ cup
    frozen processed grated hash
    brown potatoes
2 large cloves of garlic, minced
1 tablespoon vegetable oil
8 ounces feta cheese, crumbled
8 ounces peeled cooked small
    shrimp, chopped
$1/2$ cup plus 1 tablespoon
    mayonnaise
$1/2$ teaspoon chili powder
$3/4$ teaspoon ground cumin
$1/4$ cup sesame seeds
Paprika to taste

### Garnish
*Parsley leaves*
*Thin lemon slices*

☛ Slice the pitas into halves horizontally. Spread the cut sides with butter. Cut into 5 or 6 triangles.

☛ Place buttered side up on a nonstick baking sheet. Bake at 300 degrees for 15 to 20 minutes or until crisp and lightly browned.

☛ Sauté the potatoes and garlic in the oil in a skillet until heated through.

☛ Combine the cheese, shrimp, mayonnaise, potato mixture, chili powder and cumin in a medium bowl, stirring with a fork until mixed.

☛ Spread the topping over the pita triangles. Sprinkle with the sesame seeds and paprika. Broil 4 to 6 inches from the heat source for 1 to 2 minutes or until bubbly.

☛ Arrange on a parsley-lined serving plate. Garnish with lemon slices.

☛ May be frozen; reheat at 450 degrees for 5 to 8 minutes or until heated through.

### A SPELLING LESSON

If you ever wondered how to spell potato, you got the answer on 1990s' TV talk shows when a U.S. vice-presidential candidate publicly corrected an elementary student's spelling. The candidate added an incorrect "e" and became the target of many jokes, which probably didn't help his campaign much. He was defeated, and now we know it is not spelled "potatoe."

# POTATO EMPANADAS

*Yield: 12 servings*

8 medium russet potatoes, peeled, cut into cubes
¹/₂ cup butter, divided
1 cup milk
8 ounces Monterey Jack cheese, shredded
1 tablespoon flour
1 teaspoon salt
2 tablespoons instant minced onion
4 recipes (1-crust) pie pastry, or 4 unbaked pie shells
1 tablespoon dillweed
1 tablespoon mayonnaise

☞ Cook the potatoes in boiling salted water to cover in a saucepan until tender. Drain well and keep warm.

☞ Melt ¹/₄ cup of the butter in a small saucepan. Add the milk. Bring to a boil; reduce the heat. Add the cheese. Cook until the cheese is melted, stirring constantly. Stir in the flour and salt. Add the onion and mix well.

☞ Stir the cheese sauce into the potatoes, mixing gently to coat.

☞ Roll the pastry dough into a rectangle on a lightly floured surface. Cut into 5-inch squares.

☞ Place a large spoonful of the potato mixture in the center of each square. Fold each square over to form a crescent shape, sealing with a wet fork. Place on a greased baking sheet.

☞ Melt the remaining ¹/₄ cup butter in a saucepan. Mix with the dillweed and mayonnaise in a bowl. Brush over both sides of the crescents.

☞ Bake at 375 degrees for 12 to 18 minutes or until lightly browned.

## NEAPOLITAN POTATO PIZZA

*Yield: 6 to 8 servings*

*2 pounds russet potatoes*
*1 (15-ounce) can peeled tomatoes*
*Salt to taste*
*1/4 cup extra-virgin olive oil, divided*
*1/2 teaspoon freshly ground pepper*
*10 ounces mozzarella cheese, sliced*
*8 oil-pack anchovy fillets, drained,*
  *chopped*
*1 teaspoon dried oregano*
*Chopped parsley (optional)*
*1 cup sour cream (optional)*

☛ Boil the potatoes in boiling salted water to cover in a saucepan until tender.

☛ Place the tomatoes in a strainer. Sprinkle heavily with salt. Drain for 10 to 15 minutes to remove as much moisture as possible.

☛ Peel the potatoes. Force through a sieve or mash with a potato ricer. Mix with 2 tablespoons of the olive oil, additional salt and pepper in a bowl. Spread over an oiled round pizza pan. Layer the cheese, anchovies and tomatoes over the potato mixture. Sprinkle with the oregano. Drizzle with the remaining 2 tablespoons olive oil.

☛ Bake at 400 degrees for 20 minutes.

☛ Sprinkle with the parsley. Serve hot with sour cream on the side.

☛

*Note: Don't let the anchovies keep you from trying this appetizer. The potatoes absorb the salt and give it quite an unusual taste. It's a great crowd pleaser.*

☛

## POTATO STICKS

*Yield: 3 dozen*

*10 ounces frozen processed grated*
  *hash brown potatoes, thawed*
*1 1/4 cups butter, softened*
*2 1/2 cups flour*
*1 teaspoon salt*
*2 egg yolks*
*1/4 cup half-and-half*
*Coarse salt, poppy seeds or*
  *caraway seeds to taste*

☛ Mix the potatoes, butter and flour in a bowl. Stir in the salt.

☛ Knead on a lightly floured surface until the dough is smooth. Roll 2 tablespoons at a time into the shape of a breadstick. Make shallow diagonal slits in the tops of the sticks.

☛ Beat the egg yolks and half-and-half in a bowl. Brush over each potato stick. Sprinkle with coarse salt.

☛ Place the potato sticks on a baking sheet. Bake at 400 degrees for 10 to 12 minutes or until golden brown.

## CRISP POTATO SKINS AND ASSORTED TOPPERS

*Yield: 6 servings*

*3 medium russet potatoes*
  *(about 2 pounds), scrubbed*
*¼ cup melted butter*
*1 teaspoon soy sauce*
*Coarse salt (optional)*

☞ Bake the potatoes at 425 degrees for 1 hour. Let cool. Cut into quarters lengthwise; then cut into halves crosswise to form 8 sections. Scoop the pulp from each skin, leaving a ¼-inch shell; reserve the pulp for another use.

☞ Increase the oven temperature to 500 degrees.

☞ Brush both sides of each potato skin with a mixture of melted butter and soy sauce. Place on a baking sheet.

☞ Bake for 10 to 12 minutes or until crisp.

☞ Sprinkle with coarse salt. Serve alone or with the following dips.

### Tapenade

*1 cup minced pitted black olives*
*6 anchovy fillets, rinsed*
*2 tablespoons capers, drained*
*2 cloves of garlic, minced*
*2 tablespoons lemon juice*
*1 tablespoon red wine vinegar*
*¼ cup (or more) olive oil*

☞ Mash the olives, anchovies, capers and garlic together in a bowl or food processor.

☞ Stir in the lemon juice and vinegar. Beat in the olive oil gradually until the mixture is thick and smooth.

### Chutney Yogurt Sauce

*1 cup plain yogurt*
*1 tablespoon curry powder*
*1 teaspoon lemon juice*
*¼ cup minced mango chutney*

☞ Mix the yogurt, curry powder, lemon juice and chutney in a bowl.

☞ Chill thoroughly.

## Salsa

6 tomatoes, peeled, seeded, chopped
1 (4-ounce) can chopped
    green chiles
1/4 cup minced onion
1 or 2 jalapeño chiles, seeded,
    minced
1/4 cup chopped cilantro
Salt to taste

🖎 Combine the tomatoes, green chiles, onion, jalapeños, cilantro and salt in a bowl and mix well.
🖎 Chill thoroughly.

🖎

*Note: These toppers may also be used to fill Petite Potato Hors d'Oeuvres (page 26).*

🖎

## POTATO-STUFFED MUSHROOM CAPS

*Yield: 6 servings*

30 medium mushrooms, cleaned
3/4 cup mashed potatoes
1/4 cup cottage cheese
2 tablespoons dried onion soup mix
1/4 cup grated Parmesan cheese
Red lettuce leaves

🖎 Remove the stems from the mushrooms carefully. Chop the stems; set aside the caps.
🖎 Mix the stems, potatoes, cottage cheese and soup mix in a small bowl. Spoon into the mushroom caps. Arrange in a greased 10x15-inch baking pan.

🖎 Bake at 375 degrees for 10 to 15 minutes or until heated through and bubbly. Remove from the oven. Set the oven on broil.
🖎 Sprinkle the mushroom caps with the Parmesan cheese. Broil for 1 to 2 minutes or until the Parmesan cheese is lightly browned.
🖎 Serve on a red lettuce-lined platter.

🖎

*Note: Leftover mashed potatoes may be used in this recipe.*

🖎

# HERBED POTATO MUSHROOM CAKES

*Yield: 10 potato cakes*

6 medium russet potatoes
    (about 2¹/₂ pounds)
1¹/₂ teaspoons crushed
    dried marjoram
1¹/₂ teaspoons crushed
    dried tarragon
1¹/₂ teaspoons crushed dried basil
4 ounces mushrooms, any variety
2 tablespoons olive oil, divided
Salt and pepper to taste
¹/₂ cup sliced shallot
¹/₂ cup sliced leek (white and pale
    green parts only)
¹/₄ cup butter
5 ounces prosciutto, thinly sliced,
    chopped
1¹/₂ cups shredded Emmentaler or
    Gruyère cheese (about 6 ounces)

🖙 Cook the potatoes in boiling salted water to cover in a saucepan for 30 minutes or until very tender; drain. Cool for 10 minutes. Peel and mash the potatoes. Stir in the marjoram, tarragon and basil.

🖙 Brush the mushrooms with 1 tablespoon of the olive oil. Season with salt and pepper. Cook under a preheated broiler for 5 minutes or until cooked through. Chop coarsely and set aside.

🖙 Heat the remaining 1 tablespoon olive oil in a small skillet over medium-high heat. Add the shallot and leek. Sauté until translucent. Stir into the potato mixture. Adjust the seasonings. Stir in the mushrooms gently.

🖙 Shape ¹/₂ cup of the mixture at a time into a 3- to 4-inch diameter cake. At this point, the cakes may be stored in the refrigerator for 1 day.

🖙 Melt 2 tablespoons of the butter in a large skillet over medium-high heat. Add the potato cakes in batches. Cook each batch for 4 minutes per side, adding the remaining butter as needed. Remove to a lightly oiled heavy large baking sheet.

🖙 Top each cake with prosciutto and cheese. Bake at 400 degrees for 10 minutes or until the cheese melts.

🖙 Serve hot.

 # POTATO TIMBALES

*Yield: 8 servings*

3 medium russet potatoes
   (about 1 pound)
1 tablespoon butter
1 tablespoon vegetable oil
1 cup chopped onion
3/4 cup grated Parmesan cheese
3/4 cup half-and-half
6 eggs, beaten
1 tablespoon chopped fresh basil, or
   1 teaspoon dried
1/2 teaspoon salt
1/8 teaspoon pepper
1 (2-ounce) can sliced black or
   green olives
1 cup tomato sauce

## Garnish
2 tablespoons minced fresh parsley

☞ Butter generously the sides and bottoms of eight 1-cup ramekins or custard cups.

☞ Peel and coarsely grate the potatoes. Place in a bowl of cold water to cover.

☞ Heat the butter and oil in a skillet. Add the onion. Sauté slowly until tender.

☞ Drain the potatoes; pat dry with paper towels. Combine the potatoes, onion, cheese and half-and-half in a bowl and mix well. Stir in the eggs. Season with the basil, salt and pepper.

☞ Fill each ramekin 1/2 full with the potato mixture. Top each with a layer of olives. Cover with the remaining potato mixture.

☞ Place the ramekins in a shallow baking pan. Pour enough boiling water into the pan to reach 1/3 of the way up the ramekins. Bake at 375 degrees for 30 to 35 minutes or until the tops are set and the mixture pulls away from the sides of the ramekins. A knife inserted near the center should come out clean.

☞ Let stand for 5 minutes and unmold onto a plate. Spoon the tomato sauce over the timbales.

☞ Garnish with the parsley.

☞

*Note: These would be beautiful as a first course for your special holiday party.*

☞

## Almond-Crusted Potato Balls

*Yield: 4 servings*

2¼ *pounds russet potatoes, peeled,*
    *cut into* ½-*inch chunks*
*1 egg yolk*
*1 teaspoon salt*
½ *cup flour*
*1 egg, beaten*
¾ *cup bread crumbs*
*1 cup flaked almonds*
*Vegetable oil for deep-frying*

☞ Boil the potatoes in salted water to cover in a saucepan for 20 minutes; drain.

☞ Mash the potatoes until smooth. Stir in the egg yolk. Season with the salt.

☞ Shape the mixture into 1-inch balls. Coat the balls successively with the flour, egg, bread crumbs and almond flakes.

☞ Fry in oil to cover in a skillet or deep fryer for 4 minutes or until golden brown.

## Mini Potato and Mushroom Tarts

*Yield: 12 servings*

*1 pound mushrooms, finely chopped*
    *(about 2 cups)*
*2 tablespoons finely chopped shallots*
    *or green onions*
*1 to 2 tablespoons butter*
½ *teaspoon tarragon (optional)*
*Salt and pepper to taste*
¼ *cup madeira*
*2 large russet potatoes, peeled*
*1 recipe (2-crust) pie pastry, or*
    *2 unbaked pie shells*
¼ *teaspoon salt*
⅛ *teaspoon pepper*
*1 cup whipping cream*
*2 tablespoons chopped chives*

☞ Sauté the mushrooms and shallots in the butter in a saucepan over medium-high heat for 6 to 8 minutes or until the mushrooms are very lightly browned. Season with tarragon and salt and pepper to taste.

☞ Add the madeira. Boil rapidly until the liquid has evaporated and the mushroom mixture has cooked down to approximately 1 cup. Set aside.

☞ Boil the potatoes in water to cover in a saucepan for 7 minutes; drain. Grate the potatoes; they may be slightly sticky.

☞ Roll out the pastry. Fit into 12 lightly greased muffin cups. Fill each muffin cup ½ full with potatoes. Add the mushroom mixture. Top with the remaining potatoes.

☞ Stir ¼ teaspoon salt and ⅛ teaspoon pepper into the whipping cream. Pour into each muffin cup. Sprinkle with the chives.

☞ Place the muffin cups on the lowest oven rack of the oven. Bake at 400 degrees for 5 minutes. Move the muffin cups to the upper middle oven rack. Reduce the oven temperature to 325 degrees. Bake for 15 minutes or until the tops of the tarts are golden brown.

# Potato and Leek Tart

*Yield: 10 servings as appetizers*
*6 servings as a brunch entrée*

## Pastry

*1¹/₄ cups flour*
*¹/₂ teaspoon salt*
*¹/₂ cup chilled butter,*
  *cut into small pieces*
*2 to 3 tablespoons ice water*

## Filling

*3 tablespoons butter*
*3 large leeks, trimmed, thinly sliced*
*3 tablespoons whipping cream*
*¹/₄ teaspoon ground nutmeg*
*¹/₄ teaspoon salt*
*¹/₈ teaspoon pepper*

## Topping

*1 large russet potato, cooked, peeled,*
  *thinly sliced*

For the pastry, mix the flour and salt in a medium bowl. Cut in the butter with a pastry blender or 2 forks until crumbly. Add the water 1 tablespoon at a time, tossing with a fork until a soft dough forms. Shape into a ball. Chill, wrapped in plastic wrap, for 1 hour.

Roll the dough into an 11-inch circle on a floured surface. Fit the pastry into a 9-inch quiche pan or pie plate. Trim the pastry even with the edge of the pan. Chill for 30 minutes.

Prick the pastry with a fork. Line with foil and fill with pie weights or dried beans. Bake at 375 degrees for 10 minutes. Remove the foil and weights. Bake for 10 minutes longer or until the crust is firm. Cool on a wire rack.

For the filling, melt the butter in a large skillet over medium heat. Add the leeks. Cook for 10 minutes or until tender. Remove and reserve 1 cup leeks. Stir the whipping cream, nutmeg, salt and pepper into the remaining leeks in the skillet. Cook for 2 minutes or until thickened, stirring occasionally.

Spoon the filling into the crust. Top with the potato slices and reserved leeks, arranging the potatoes in the center and the leeks at the edge.

Bake at 400 degrees for 10 to 15 minutes or until the filling is heated through. Cool slightly on a wire rack.

*Note: You may use a purchased prepared pie crust in this recipe or your own favorite pastry recipe.*

# OVEN-CRISPED POTATO FOCACCIA

*Yield: 8 to 10 servings as appetizers*
*6 to 8 servings as a side dish*

*$1/3$ cup oil-cured black olives,*
*    pitted, chopped*
*3 tablespoons grated orange peel*
*$1^1/4$ pounds red potatoes,*
*    thinly sliced*
*1 onion, cut into halves,*
*    thinly sliced*
*$1/4$ cup chopped fresh Italian parsley*
*3 tablespoons olive oil*
*2 cloves of garlic, minced*
*$1/2$ teaspoon crumbled dried oregano*
*$1/8$ teaspoon crushed dried*
*    red pepper*
*Salt and black pepper to taste*

☞ Mix the olives and orange peel in a small bowl.

☞ Mix the potatoes, onion, parsley, olive oil, garlic, oregano and red pepper in a large bowl. Add half the olive mixture and toss well. Season with salt and black pepper. This mixture may be prepared up to 45 minutes ahead; cover and let stand at room temperature.

☞ Spread the potato mixture evenly on an oiled pizza pan. Bake at 500 degrees for 15 minutes or until the potatoes are almost tender. Sprinkle with the remaining olive mixture. Bake for 10 minutes longer or until the potatoes are tender and just golden brown.

☞ Cut into wedges to serve.

 **ASY KNISHES**

*Yield: 12 servings*

*8 ounces russet potatoes,*
*    peeled, diced*
*1 cup thinly sliced scallions*
*Salt and pepper to taste*
*8 ounces purchased puff*
*    pastry dough*

🖐 Boil the potatoes with salted water to cover in a saucepan for 15 minutes or until tender. Drain and mash to make approximately 2 cups.

🖐 Add the scallions to the potatoes and mix well. Season with salt and pepper. Let stand until cool.

🖐 Divide the dough into halves. Place 1 half in the refrigerator. Roll the remaining dough into a 12x18-inch rectangle on a lightly floured pastry cloth or other surface. Place on a baking sheet. Chill for 30 minutes or until firm. Repeat the process with the remaining dough.

🖐 Cut each dough rectangle into six 6x6-inch pieces. Stack the pieces, placing waxed paper between each layer. Place in the refrigerator, removing 1 piece at a time as needed.

🖐 For each knish, mound 2 tablespoons well-packed potato mixture in the upper half of the rectangle. Brush the outer $^1/_8$ inch of the pastry lightly with water. Fold the pastry over the potato stuffing, sealing the edges by pushing down with the back of a fork.

🖐 Place the knishes on a parchment-lined baking sheet. Chill until baking time. The knishes may be prepared several hours ahead.

🖐 Bake at 350 degrees for 30 minutes or until golden brown, turning once.

🖐 Serve warm.

### POTATO TRIVIA

The potato is the only vegetable that grows in the desert or in mountainous areas above 14,000 feet.

## $\mathcal{P}$ETITE POTATO HORS D'OEUVRES

*Yield: 4 servings*

*12 small red potatoes*

🍃 Prepare the potatoes using 1 of the following 3 methods.

🍃 1) Scrub the potatoes and sprinkle with water. Pierce with a fork. Place on a microwave-safe dish and cover with vented plastic wrap. Microwave on High for 8 to 12 minutes or until almost done; the potatoes will continue to cook for several minutes after removal from the microwave. Let stand for 3 to 4 minutes. Cut into halves.

🍃 2) Cut the potatoes into halves. Toss with 1 tablespoon olive oil. Place cut side down on a baking sheet. Bake at 350 degrees for 25 minutes or until tender.

🍃 3) Boil the potatoes in salted water for 15 to 20 minutes or until tender. Cut into halves and let cool.

🍃 Cut a small slice off the rounded end of each potato half so that the potatoes stand upright. Remove a small scoop from the top of each with a small spoon or melon baller. Spoon the filling into the cavities.

### Smoked Salmon Filling
*3¹/₂ ounces smoked salmon, finely chopped*
*2 tablespoons sour cream*
*2 tablespoons minced red onion*
*1 teaspoon capers, drained*
*¹/₂ teaspoon prepared white horseradish*
*Pepper to taste*

🍃 Mix the salmon, sour cream, onion, capers, horseradish and pepper in a bowl. Chill thoroughly. Spoon 1 teaspoon filling into each potato half at serving time.

🍃 The potatoes and the topping may be prepared up to 1 day ahead and stored separately in the refrigerator.

### Sour Cream and Green Onion Filling
*1 cup sour cream, low-fat sour cream or nonfat sour cream*
*4 green onions, finely chopped*
*¹/₄ teaspoon dried oregano, or to taste*

🍃 Mix the sour cream, green onions and oregano in a bowl. Spoon into the potatoes.

### Sour Cream and Chive Filling
*¹/₂ cup sour cream*
*1 tablespoon prepared white horseradish*
*3 tablespoons chopped black olives*
*2 tablespoons finely chopped chives or green onions*

🍃 Mix the sour cream, horseradish, olives and chives in a bowl. Spoon into the potatoes. Serve over a bed of salad greens.

### Sour Cream and Caviar Filling
*1¹/₂ cups vodka*
*1 cup sour cream or low-fat sour cream*
*1 (1¹/₂-ounce) jar red or black caviar*

🍃 Spoon 1 tablespoon vodka into each potato cavity. Top with a dollop of sour cream. Sprinkle with caviar.

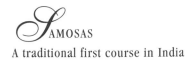

# Samosas
### A traditional first course in India

*Yield: 8 servings (3 samosas per person)*

## Dough
*1¹/₂ cups whole wheat flour*
*1¹/₂ cups all-purpose flour*
*1 teaspoon salt*
*¹/₂ teaspoon ground turmeric*
*¹/₄ cup butter or margarine*
*³/₄ to 1 cup water*

## Filling
*2 cups plus 1 to 2 tablespoons water, divided*
*3 cups diced unpeeled potatoes*
*1¹/₂ cups plus 2 tablespoons vegetable oil, divided*
*³/₄ cup finely chopped onion*
*³/₄ cup diced carrot*
*2 teaspoons minced peeled garlic*
*2 teaspoons minced peeled ginger*
*1 teaspoon mustard seeds*
*¹/₂ teaspoon ground turmeric*
*1 teaspoon curry powder*
*1 teaspoon ground coriander*
*¹/₁₆ to ¹/₈ teaspoon cayenne*
*1 teaspoon salt*
*1 cup fresh or frozen peas*
*2 teaspoons fresh lemon juice*

☞ For the dough, combine the whole wheat flour, all-purpose flour, salt, turmeric and butter in a food processor. Pulse until the mixture becomes crumbly. Add the water gradually, pulsing until a smooth dough forms. This process may be performed with a mixer instead of a food processor.

☞ Turn the dough onto a floured surface. Knead by hand or with a dough hook for 5 to 10 minutes or until smooth. Chill, covered, for 2 hours. At this point, the dough may be stored in the refrigerator overnight; let stand at room temperature for 1 hour before using.

☞ For the filling, bring 2 cups water to a boil in a saucepan. Add the potatoes. Cook for 10 minutes or just until tender; drain and set aside.

☞ Heat 2 tablespoons of the oil in a large skillet over medium heat. Add the onion, carrot, garlic, ginger and mustard seeds. Sauté for 5 minutes or until the vegetables are tender, adding the remaining 1 to 2 tablespoons water if the ginger begins to stick. Remove from the heat. Stir in the potatoes, turmeric, curry powder, coriander, cayenne, salt, peas and lemon juice.

☞ Turn the dough onto a floured surface. Roll ¹/₁₆ to ¹/₈ inch thick. Cut into circles with a 5-inch round bowl or jar lid. Continue to reroll and cut circles until all the dough is used; there should be about 24 circles.

☞ Spread 2 tablespoons of the filling in the center of a dough circle. Beginning at the bottom of the circle, bring each side edge together ²/₃ of the way up to form an ice cream cone shape. Fold down the top of the circle. Pinch the edges to the top of the cone to seal into a triangle-shaped packet. Repeat with the remaining dough and filling.

☞ Heat the remaining 1¹/₂ cups oil in a small deep saucepan over medium-high heat until a bit of dough dropped into the oil sizzles and bubbles to the top immediately. Fry the somosas 1 at a time for 2 to 3 minutes per side or until golden brown. Set each aside and keep warm.

☞ Serve with chutney and yogurt.

# Brunch & BREAKFAST

## Potato Gleanings

In the fall of 1863 farmer Seth Jones grew 54,000 pounds of potatoes on his new farm near Mt. Idaho, Idaho County. He sold them to miners for eight cents per pound.

In 1877 the *Idaho Statesman* claimed that Boise valley was the best potato country anywhere. I. P. Guile grew *White Mechanic,* and *Kidney* or *Bread* potatoes at the mouth of Mores' Creek.

In 1881 the Idaho potato was praised as "the most thoroughly American of all vegetables." The *Idaho Statesman* predicted that in years ahead "from here to Farewell Bend, their modest blue blossoms shall wave over thousands of acres tilled by industrious and intelligent farmers. And a hungry world shall wag its limber jaws over their mealy lining and bless the name of Idaho." The author waxed even more poetic: "And what a truly modest creature it is, in its sober russet coat and its snowy interior, with the grateful steam ascending from the plate to tickle the nostrils and bewilder the palate."

In September, 1881, A. H. Vaughn was raising "the largest, smoothest and handsomest potatoes that we have seen in many a day… He left one of his spuds at Jimmy Hart's saloon that weighs five pounds." By 1881 potatoes were selling for only a cent a pound, and without a railroad in southern Idaho there was no way to get them to a larger market.

In 1924, although farm prices were generally down, Idaho farmers were shipping potatoes to 33 states. The Los Angeles area alone received 2585 carloads of Idaho's now famous potatoes, Chicago 1163 carloads.

In 1934, a Depression year, a common complaint still heard today surfaced: "Why do Idahoans eat the culls and seconds while all the best potatoes are shipped out of state?" The reason was economic, of course. The best potatoes sold for fifteen cents a pound in big cities—Idahoans got the two-cent ones.

The slogan "Famous Potatoes" first appeared on Idaho license plates in 1948.

Missionary Henry Harmon Spalding grew the first potato crop in what is now Idaho in 1836 near the confluence of Lapwai Creek and the Clearwater River. He and other early missionaries tried to get the Indians to give up their seasonal migrations and to settle down as farmers.

Famous Shoshoni leader Washakie, after listening to a white man's harangue about the advantages of his becoming a farmer, is reputed to have made a short but clear response. He said only "God damn a potato!"

— *by Arthur A. Hart, Historian*

# Farmer's Casserole

*Yield: 6 to 8 servings*

*1 tablespoon olive oil*
*4 cups potatoes, cut into*
　　*¹/₂-inch cubes*
*³/₄ cup shredded*
　　*Monterey Jack cheese*
*1 cup diced cooked ham or*
　　*Canadian bacon*
*¹/₄ cup sliced green onions*
*1 jalapeño pepper, seeded,*
　　*finely chopped*
*4 eggs, beaten, or 1 cup*
　　*egg substitute*
*¹/₂ cup milk*
*¹/₄ teaspoon pepper*

☞ Grease a 2-quart square baking dish with the olive oil. Arrange the potatoes evenly in the dish. Bake at 350 degrees for 10 minutes.

☞ Stir the potatoes. Sprinkle with the cheese, ham, green onions and jalapeño.

☞ Mix the eggs, milk and pepper in a bowl. Pour over the potatoes. At this point, the casserole may be covered and stored in the refrigerator overnight.

☞ Bake, uncovered, at 350 degrees for 40 to 45 minutes or until the potatoes are tender.

☞ Serve with fresh fruit.

# Huevos California

*Yield: 1 serving*

*1 tablespoon butter or margarine*
*¹/₂ cup frozen Ore-Ida*
　　*Potatoes O'Brien*
*¹/₄ teaspoon salt*
*¹/₄ teaspoon chili powder*
*2 eggs, beaten*
*1 (9-inch) flour tortilla*
*2 tablespoons sour cream*
*1 tablespoon taco sauce (optional)*
*1 teaspoon chopped green onions*

## Garnish
*Sour cream*
*Chopped green onions*

☞ Melt the butter in a skillet over medium heat. Add the Potatoes O'Brien, salt and chili powder. Cook until the potatoes are tender, stirring occasionally. Add the eggs. Scramble until set.

☞ Warm the tortilla briefly in a dry skillet over very low heat, turning frequently.

☞ Spoon the egg mixture onto the tortilla. Top with the sour cream, taco sauce and green onions. Fold up the sides like an envelope and roll up.

☞ Garnish with sour cream and green onions.

# DOVER POTATOES
## (DOUGH OVER POTATOES)

*Yield: 4 to 6 servings*

*2 cups flour*
*1 teaspoon baking powder*
*1 teaspoon salt*
*2 eggs*
*1³/₄ cups milk*
*¹/₂ cup vegetable oil*
*3 to 4 medium russet potatoes,*
*    cooked, cut into 1-inch cubes*

🖎 For the dough, combine the flour, baking powder, salt, eggs, milk and ¹/₄ cup of the oil in a large bowl and mix well.

🖎 Heat the remaining ¹/₄ cup oil in a 10-inch skillet. Add the potatoes. Fry until the potatoes are crisp and heated through.

🖎 Pour the dough over the potatoes. Scramble as for eggs, breaking up the dough into smaller pieces with a spatula. Fry until the dough is cooked through.

🖎 Serve with dark corn syrup.

🖎

*This recipe was developed to use up leftover potatoes. When the son of the cook inquired what she was serving, the cook replied, "Dough over potatoes." Upon being asked at school one day to tell about his favorite breakfast, the boy told them it was Dover Potatoes. The name stuck, and the dish has been known that way ever since. There were many mornings when the children were rousted from bed hearing "Dover Potatoes!!" and they would race to get their fair share. It's great to take camping, too!*

🖎

# OTATO SAUSAGE TART

*Yield: 6 to 8 servings*

1 unbaked (9-inch) tart shell or
    pie shell
1 pound mild or hot Italian sausage
2 cups cream-style cottage cheese
2 eggs
2¼ cups well-seasoned warm
    mashed potatoes
½ cup sour cream
1 teaspoon dried oregano
Salt and pepper to taste
2 tablespoons melted butter
2 cups shredded Cheddar cheese

## Garnish
*Cherry tomatoes, cut into halves*

🖝 Bake the tart shell at 450 degrees for 7 minutes. Set aside. Reduce the oven temperature to 350 degrees.

🖝 Remove the casing from the sausage. Crumble the sausage into a skillet. Cook until cooked through; drain on paper towels.

🖝 Combine the cottage cheese and eggs in a blender container or food processor container. Process until blended. Pour into a large bowl. Beat in the potatoes, sour cream, oregano, salt and pepper.

🖝 Place the sausage in the tart shell. Spoon the potato mixture over the sausage. Brush the top with the butter. Sprinkle with the cheese.

🖝 Bake for 50 to 60 minutes or until heated through.

🖝 Just before serving, arrange the tomato halves cut side down around the outer edge of the tart.

## POTATO TRIVIA

A large baked

potato has twice the

potassium of a

medium banana.

## Holiday Breakfast Hash

From Ore-Ida Foods, Inc.

*Yield: 6 to 8 servings*

8 ounces sausage, chopped
8 ounces bacon, chopped
$^1/_2$ cup Ore-Ida Chopped Onions
$2^1/_2$ cups frozen Ore-Ida
   Potatoes O'Brien
6 eggs, beaten
1 (4-ounce) can asparagus, drained
1 tomato, chopped
Grated Parmesan cheese

☞ Cook the sausage and bacon in a skillet until cooked through; drain partially. Add the onions. Sauté until the onions are translucent.

☞ Add the Potatoes O'Brien. Cook until the potatoes are browned. Add the eggs and mix well. Stir in the asparagus and tomato. Top with the cheese.

## Sweet Potato Scrambled Eggs

*Yield: 4 servings*

$1^1/_2$ cups diced sweet potatoes
4 slices bacon, chopped
6 large eggs, beaten
1 teaspoon ground red chiles
$^1/_4$ teaspoon salt
2 green onions with tops, sliced

☞ Bring enough salted water to a boil in a saucepan to cover the sweet potatoes; use approximately $^1/_4$ teaspoon salt per 1 cup water. Add the sweet potatoes. Cover and return to a boil; reduce the heat. Simmer for 6 minutes or until tender; drain.

☞ Cook the bacon in a 10-inch skillet until crisp; drain the skillet, reserving 1 tablespoon drippings. Drain the bacon on paper towels.

☞ Cook the potatoes in the reserved drippings in the skillet over medium heat until golden brown, stirring frequently.

☞ Mix the eggs, ground chiles and salt in a bowl. Pour into the skillet. Sprinkle the mixture with the bacon and green onions. Scramble for 3 to 5 minutes or until the eggs are cooked through but still moist. (As the mixture begins to set on the bottom and sides, raise it so that the uncooked mixture flows underneath the cooked mixture.)

## Easy Hash Brown Quiche

*Yield: 4 to 6 servings*

*3 cups frozen country-style hash*
   *brown potatoes, thawed*
*¹/₄ cup melted butter*
*1 cup finely chopped cooked ham*
*1 cup shredded Cheddar cheese*
*¹/₄ cup chopped green bell pepper*
*¹/₄ cup sliced green onions*
*3 eggs*
*¹/₂ cup milk*
*Salt and pepper to taste*

🖝 Form the potatoes into a shell in a quiche pan or pie plate. Drizzle with the butter. Bake at 425 degrees for 25 minutes. Remove from the oven.

🖝 Decrease the oven temperature to 350 degrees.

🖝 Mix the ham, cheese, green pepper and green onions in a bowl. Spread over the potatoes.

🖝 Beat the eggs, milk, salt and pepper in a bowl. Pour over the ham mixture.

🖝 Bake for 30 minutes or until a knife inserted near the center comes out clean.

🖝 Let stand for 10 minutes before cutting.

### BETTER HOMEMADE HASH BROWNS

After shredding your potatoes, rinse or soak them in cold water. Then drain and pat them dry. This process will remove the potato starch that causes the potatoes to stick and slows the browning.

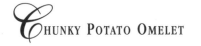

# CHUNKY POTATO OMELET

*Yield: 1 serving*

*¹/₂ small onion, chopped*
*1 tablespoon butter*
*²/₃ cup cubed potato, cooked*
*2 eggs, beaten*
*Salt and pepper to taste*
*2 slices bacon, crisp-fried, crumbled*
*1 teaspoon finely chopped chives*

🖜 Sauté the onion in the butter in a skillet. Stir in the potato and set aside.

🖜 Beat the eggs, salt and pepper in a bowl.

🖜 Place a skillet coated with nonstick cooking spray over medium heat. Pour in the egg mixture; reduce the heat to low. Cook for 1 minute.

🖜 Sprinkle the potato mixture over the egg mixture and mix well. Cook until set.

🖜 Sprinkle the bacon and chives over the top.

🖜 Fold the omelet in half. Slide from the skillet onto a serving plate.

# HOBO HASH

*Yield: 6 servings*

8 eggs
*¹/₄ cup cottage cheese*
*1 small onion, chopped*
*1 (12-ounce) package frozen*
*    shredded hash brown potatoes*
*2 tablespoons vegetable oil*
*Salt and pepper to taste*
*4 ounces Cheddar cheese, shredded*

## Garnish
*2 tablespoons chopped chives or*
*    green onions*

🍃 Beat the eggs and cottage cheese in a bowl.

🍃 Sauté the onion and potatoes in the oil in a large nonstick skillet until golden brown. Add the egg mixture. Season with salt and pepper. Cook until the eggs are firm, stirring constantly.

🍃 Sprinkle with the cheese. Garnish with the chives. May serve with sour cream and/or salsa.

🍃

*Note: May add 1 pound cooked ground sausage to the skillet at the same time as the egg mixture.*

🍃

# SMOKED SALMON HASH

*Yield: 4 to 5 servings*

*8 ounces firm smoked salmon or*
*    trout, skinned, boned*
*¹/₃ cup sour cream or reduced-fat*
*    sour cream*
*3 tablespoons capers, drained*
*2 tablespoons prepared horseradish*
*2 tablespoons minced parsley*
*1 tablespoon lemon juice*
*1 small red onion, finely chopped*
*1 teaspoon minced garlic*
*¹/₄ cup butter or margarine*
*3 cups frozen hash brown potatoes*

## Garnish
*2 tablespoons sliced green onions*
*Reduced-fat sour cream*
*Freshly ground pepper to taste*

🍃 Shred the salmon into a large bowl. Add the sour cream, capers, horseradish, parsley and lemon juice and mix gently.

🍃 Cook the red onion and garlic in 1 tablespoon of the butter in a 10- to 12-inch nonstick skillet for 5 minutes or until the onion is translucent. Stir into the salmon mixture.

🍃 Melt the remaining 3 tablespoons butter in a skillet over medium heat. Add the potatoes. Cook, covered, for 12 to 15 minutes or until the potatoes are browned on the bottom and tender; stir. Cook, uncovered, over medium-high heat for 5 minutes or until deep golden brown, stirring occasionally. Remove from the heat.

🍃 Scrape the salmon mixture onto the potatoes. Mix gently and pat into an even layer. Cook over medium heat for 10 minutes or until well browned and crusty, turning portions occasionally with a spatula.

🍃 Spoon the hash onto plates. Garnish with green onions, sour cream and pepper.

🍃

*Note: This dish is naturally salty, so no additional salt is needed.*

🍃

# Cauliflower Cheese Pie

*Yield: 6 servings*

### Potato Crust
*2 cups grated potatoes*
*½ teaspoon salt*
*¼ cup grated onion*

### Cauliflower Filling
*1 teaspoon minced garlic*
*1 cup chopped onion*
*3 tablespoons olive oil*
*1 medium head cauliflower*
*  or broccoli, broken into*
*  small pieces*
*½ teaspoon basil*
*Salt and pepper to taste*
*1 cup shredded sharp Cheddar*
*  cheese or ½ cup each Monterey*
*  Jack cheese and Cheddar cheese*
*2 eggs*
*¼ cup milk*

### Garnish
*Paprika to taste*

✒ For the crust, place the potatoes in a colander in the sink and press to remove any excess water. Add the salt and onion and mix well.

✒ Spoon the potato mixture into an oiled 9-inch pie plate. Spread thinly around the pie plate and press over the side.

✒ Bake at 400 degrees for 30 minutes. Brush the crust with a small amount of oil to make the crust crispy. Bake for 10 to 15 minutes longer or until golden brown.

✒ For the filling, sauté the garlic and onion in the olive oil in a skillet until translucent. Add the cauliflower and basil. Sauté for 10 minutes. Season with salt and pepper.

✒ Spread half the cheese over the baked crust. Cover with the filling. Top with the remaining cheese.

✒ Blend the eggs and milk in a bowl. Pour over the cheese. Garnish with paprika for color.

✒ Bake at 375 degrees for 35 minutes.

✒ Serve with a salad and foccacia bread.

# Potato Tomato Pie

*Yield: 6 to 8 servings*

3 russet potatoes
2 ready-made pie pastries
4 large ripe tomatoes, chopped
1 small white onion, diced
³/₄ cup mayonnaise
2 cups shredded Cheddar cheese
¹/₄ cup loosely packed fresh basil, or
   1 tablespoon dried
Salt and pepper to taste

## Garnish
*Paprika to taste*
*Minced parsley to taste*

☞ Parboil the potatoes in a saucepan. Let cool. Peel and cut into ¹/₈-inch slices.

☞ Fit 1 pie pastry into a greased pie plate. Bake at 375 degrees for 7 minutes. Set aside.

☞ Combine the tomatoes, onion, mayonnaise, cheese, basil, salt and pepper in a bowl and mix well. Spoon half the mixture into the pie shell. Arrange the potato slices over the tomato mixture. Top with the remaining tomato mixture.

☞ Cover with the remaining pastry. Garnish each quarter alternately with paprika and parsley.

☞ Cover the outer edge of the pastry with strips of foil to prevent overbaking.

☞ Bake at 375 degrees for 25 minutes. Remove the foil. Bake for 35 minutes longer or until the crust is browned and the filling is bubbly.

☞ Let cool for 30 minutes before cutting.

## Removing a Broken Light Bulb

Have you ever noticed

how hard it is to

unscrew a light bulb

when the bulb has

broken but its socket

still remains? Try

putting a raw potato

into the bulb's base

and twisting it. The

broken bulb should

come out with

no problem.

## Breakfast Pizza

*Yield: 6 to 8 servings*

1 (8-count) can crescent rolls
1 pound sausage
2 cups frozen hash brown potatoes,
    thawed
5 eggs, beaten
¹/₄ cup milk
Salt and pepper to taste
1¹/₂ cups shredded mozzarella cheese
    or Cheddar cheese

🐦 Press the rolls onto a 14-inch pizza pan, pressing to seal the perforations.

🐦 Brown the sausage in a skillet, stirring until crumbly; drain.

🐦 Layer the sausage and potatoes over the rolls.

🐦 Mix the eggs, milk, salt and pepper in a bowl. Pour over the potatoes. Sprinkle with the cheese.

🐦 Bake at 350 degrees for 35 to 45 minutes or until bubbly and lightly browned.

🐦

*Note: For a change of flavor, spread some spaghetti sauce or pizza sauce over the rolls.*

🐦

## Potato Oat Pancakes
A delicious low-fat recipe

*Yield: 3 to 4 servings (10 pancakes)*

³/₄ cup oat flour or
    whole wheat flour
¹/₂ cup instant potato flakes
¹/₄ cup rolled oats
3 tablespoons oat bran
1 teaspoon baking powder
¹/₂ teaspoon cinnamon
2 egg whites, or 1 egg
1 banana, mashed
1 cup skim milk

🐦 Mix the flour, potato flakes, oats, oat bran, baking powder and cinnamon in a bowl. Add the egg whites, banana and skim milk and mix well.

🐦 Pour the batter onto a greased griddle or skillet. Cook for 2 to 3 minutes per side.

🐦 Serve hot with fresh fruit, applesauce or pancake syrup.

🐦

*Note: This batter may also be prepared in a blender. It should yield approximately ten 4-inch pancakes.*

🐦

# Mashed Potato Waffles

*Yield: 4 servings*

*1¹/₂ cups flour*
*2 teaspoons baking powder*
*1 teaspoon baking soda*
*1¹/₂ teaspoons salt*
*³/₄ teaspoon freshly ground pepper*
*¹/₄ cup vegetable oil*
*1¹/₂ cups mashed cooked potatoes*
*1¹/₂ cups buttermilk*
*3 eggs, lightly beaten*
*8 slices bacon, crisp-fried, crumbled*
*3 green onions, finely chopped*

🖝 Combine the flour, baking powder, baking soda, salt and pepper in a large bowl and mix well.

🖝 Blend the oil into the potatoes in a medium bowl. Add the buttermilk gradually. Add the eggs, beating until fairly smooth.

🖝 Stir the bacon and green onions into the flour mixture. Add the potato mixture and mix well.

🖝 Oil lightly a preheated waffle iron. Pour in enough batter for 1 batch. Spread with a spatula and close the waffle iron. Cook until the waffle iron opens easily and the waffles are crisp.

🖝 Keep the finished waffles warm in a 250-degree oven while cooking the remaining batter.

### Tidbits

Potato historians have noted that when Marie Antoinette said of her peasant subjects, "Let them eat cake," she actually meant, "Let them eat potato cakes."

## POTATO TRIVIA

Russia grows more

potatoes than any

other country.

# BREAKFAST
## POTATO PANCAKES

From *Bound to Please*,
Junior League of Boise, 1983

*Yield: 4 servings*

*4 eggs*
*²/₃ cup flour*
*1¹/₂ teaspoons salt*
*2 tablespoons bacon drippings or*
  *vegetable oil*
*¹/₂ cup milk*
*¹/₂ small onion, diced*
*2 cups diced peeled potatoes*
*1 teaspoon ascorbic acid*
*Butter*
*Sour cream with chives*

☞ Beat the eggs in a blender until frothy. Add the flour, salt, bacon drippings, milk, onion, potatoes and ascorbic acid in the order listed. Blend briefly until the potatoes are shredded. Shape into 4 patties.

☞ Bake on a hot grill for 2 minutes per side, turning only once. Do not stack.

☞ Top with butter and sour cream.

☞ This is great for breakfast with bacon and applesauce.

## OURDOUGH FLAPJACKS

*Yield: 3 to 4 servings (10 flapjacks)*

2 cups Sourdough Starter
2 tablespoons sugar
*¼ cup vegetable oil*
1 egg
*½ teaspoon salt*
1 teaspoon baking soda

☞ Combine the Sourdough Starter, sugar, oil, egg and salt in a medium bowl. Add the baking soda, stirring gently just until mixed; do not beat. The batter will thicken.

☞ Bake on a lightly oiled medium-hot grill for 2 to 3 minutes or until both sides are bubbly and browned. Serve immediately.

## Sourdough Starter

*1 medium potato, peeled, cubed*
*3 cups water*
*2 cups flour*
*1 tablespoon sugar*
*1 envelope active dry yeast*

☞ Boil the potato in the water in a saucepan for 15 minutes or until very tender. Mash the potato in the cooking liquid. Beat until very smooth.

☞ Cool the potato mixture to 98 degrees. Stir in the flour, sugar and yeast. Mix until creamy. Let stand at room temperature for 2 to 4 days before using, stirring once each day.

☞ To store, always leave a small amount of batter in the sourdough pot to get the next batch started.

☞ To replenish, add 1 tablespoon sugar and equal parts flour and lukewarm water. Stir until creamy. Let it stand and bubble before using.

☞ After the initial brewing period of 2 to 4 days, store the starter, uncovered, in the refrigerator, pouring off some and replenishing it if not used every week or two.

## SOURDOUGH TIPS

A good sourdough starter is cherished like gold! Always keep your starter in a glass or crockery jar, not plastic or metal. If there is water on top of your starter, just fold it back into the starter; don't pour it off. If a crust develops on top, let the starter stand at room temperature and the crust will dissolve back into the starter. Salt kills a sourdough starter. Do not use self-rising flour.

Potato Digger and Sorter
J. B. Keeler Ranch
2 Mile East Twin Falls, Idaho
300 Bu. Per Acre.

Bisbee Photo.

# Breads

## FAMOUS IDAHO RESORTS

### COEUR D'ALENE

Just 110 miles south of the Canadian border is Coeur d'Alene,
a city and resort on the shores of the large lake that bears
the same name. Lake Coeur d'Alene has more than 135 miles
of shoreline and 16 miles of clear water. But that is not the

area's only lake. Within a 60-mile radius there are at least 60 more, most of them surrounded by lush forests.

The name's origin is interesting. Early French Canadian traders called the local tribe Coeur d'Alene. The French thought the Indians used sharp trading practices, so they gave them a name that means "heart like an awl" for the sharp-pointed tool.

The Indians were Christianized by the Jesuit priests in the 1840s. By 1853, Father Ravalli was well along in leading them toward completion of the Sacred Heart Mission overlooking the Coeur d'Alene River. This is Idaho's oldest building, a national monument often known as the Cataldo Mission.

The United States built Fort Sherman at the headwaters of the Spokane River in 1879 and established the pioneer village that eventually became Coeur d'Alene.

Then came the miners! Gold was discovered near the North Fork of the Coeur d'Alene River in 1883. The next year miners found silver to the south near Wallace. Steamboats used the lakes and rivers as highways to move supplies to the mines and to lumber camps. They were a great

way to float logs to local mills before they were shipped to market on the new transcontinental railroad.

Wallace became the hub of one of the richest mining districts in the world. To date, miners have extracted over $5 billion worth of metals from this area. Many of the town's buildings have been preserved and are on the National Register of Historic Places. Here is a chance to see the Old West as it was in the territory's early days.

Today, the Coeur d'Alene area is known as the "Playground of the Northwest" and hosts hiking, downhill skiing, hundreds of miles of cross-country skiing and snowmobile trails, plus plenty more outdoor adventures. One golf course features a moveable green that floats in the lake!

As a sparkling jewel of the Gem State, Coeur d'Alene is a year-round vacation spot.

## McCall

Travel one hundred miles north of Boise via a scenic highway to McCall, one of the most popular destinations for residents of the capital city and for tourists. The town is perched on the edge of Payette Lake, a large glacial lake surrounded by mountains and forests.

First to enjoy the bounties of the McCall area were the Nez Perce,

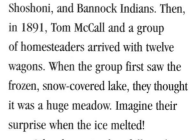

Shoshoni, and Bannock Indians. Then, in 1891, Tom McCall and a group of homesteaders arrived with twelve wagons. When the group first saw the frozen, snow-covered lake, they thought it was a huge meadow. Imagine their surprise when the ice melted!

Other homesteaders followed, along with cattlemen and sheepmen. The ranchers tried to prevent settlers from taking the prime Long Valley land, so the settlers posted armed guards at local bridges and ferries to prevent sheep and cattle from coming into the valley. Range wars, with several deaths, followed.

The range wars ended when the Forest Service stepped in. Local historians credit the Forest Service with opening the countryside to settlers by building roads and providing other public benefits.

Besides ranching, logging has had a long history of influence on the local economy. Loggers cut timber for the local mills from the nearby Payette and Boise National Forest lands.

Today, McCall is known as Ski Town USA because McCall winter athletes have competed in all but four of the Winter Olympic games. There is excellent downhill skiing in powder snow at Brundage Mountain Ski Area.

There are lots of trails for cross-country skiing and snowmobiling.

One of the most festive events is the annual Winter Carnival. There are countless activities and contests during this week. One of the most popular is the ice sculpture contest, when teams compete outdoors to see who can build the biggest and best. The streets of McCall are lined with frozen fantasies that could be straight out of Disneyland.

Summer at 5,000 feet in McCall is an Alpine experience that visitors relish. Water sports such as sailing, water-skiing, and canoeing are world class. There are thrilling whitewater rafting trips on the Salmon and Payette Rivers. Scenic drives, backpacking, camping, golf, or just enjoying sunny days at the beach are part of the wonderful McCall activities.

## SUN VALLEY

America's first grand-destination ski resort was Sun Valley, and today it maintains its reputation worldwide as a premier resort. Sun Valley is in South Central Idaho, just three hours from Boise in the Northern Rockies.

The concept of a destination ski resort began in the 1930s when Averell Harriman, later Board Chairman of Union Pacific Railroad, wanted to turn the snows of the West into an asset for the railroad. He was a longtime skier who was impressed by the Swiss ski resorts of St. Moritz and Gstaad, and he wanted to build something like them in this country.

So in 1932, Harriman hired an Austrian, Count Felix Schaffgotsch, to find the perfect spot. The count's odyssey took him to many sites, but he could not find one with all the necessary elements.

Just as Count Schaffgotsch was about to abandon his search, he learned of an old mining town called Ketchum, Idaho. Guided by a local boy, the count soon fell under the area's enchantment. He wired Harriman: "This combines more delightful features than any place I have seen in the United States, Switzerland, or Austria for a winter resort."

Harriman visited, immediately purchased the 4,300-acre Brass Ranch, and began building his lodge, recruiting the finest architects. He set the railroad's engineering department in motion to produce the world's first chairlift, using a design based on a hoist used to haul bananas into ships' holds.

With the geography squared away and the physical infrastructure on its way, Harriman hired Steve Hannagan, a public relations whiz, to publicize the area. Hannagan coined the name Sun Valley. He and Harriman agreed that it would be an elegant resort where guests could "rough it" in style. They invited socialites and movie stars to the opening of Sun Valley Lodge on December 21, 1936, gathering head-lines across the country.

What took Nature millions of years to make and Harriman's money to develop became an instant success.

Sun Valley is now a timeless resort for all seasons. Nestled in the rugged Sawtooth Mountains, the base elevation is only 6,000 feet, assuring easy breathing for people of all ages. It is a paradise for hikers, bicyclists, fly-fishermen, kayakers, and cross-country and downhill skiers. Bald Mountain, lovingly called Baldy, provides a consistent 3,400-foot vertical drop, allowing skiers to ski all the way down. Olympians abound, while beginners find the broad, treeless slopes of Dollar Mountain ideal. Among the golf courses are two championship courses designed by Robert Trent Jones, Jr. Sun Valley also has a continuous outdoor ice skating rink, with ice shows often highlighted by many fine Olympic skaters.

# SOURDOUGH POTATO WHEAT BREAD

*Yield: 3 loaves*

*1 cup Sourdough Starter (page 43)*
*1¹/₂ cups very warm (105 to 110 degrees) water*
*¹/₂ cup vegetable oil*
*¹/₄ cup sugar*
*2 teaspoons salt*
*3 cups bread flour*
*3 cups whole wheat flour*
*1 teaspoon minced fresh rosemary, or ¹/₂ teaspoon dried*
*1 teaspoon minced fresh marjoram, or ¹/₂ teaspoon dried*
*1 teaspoon minced fresh thyme, or ¹/₂ teaspoon dried*
*1 teaspoon minced fresh oregano, or ¹/₂ teaspoon dried*

🍃 Combine the Sourdough Starter, water, oil, sugar and salt in a large nonmetallic bowl and mix well.

🍃 Stir in the bread flour and whole wheat flour 1 cup at a time, beating well after each addition until a stiff dough forms.

🍃 Place the dough in a large oiled bowl, turning the dough to grease the surface. Cover loosely with a damp cloth or plastic wrap sprayed with nonstick cooking spray.

🍃 Let rise in a warm (80 to 85 degrees) place for 8 to 12 hours or until doubled in bulk.

🍃 Mix the rosemary, marjoram, thyme and oregano in a small bowl.

🍃 Punch the dough down and divide into 3 equal portions. Roll 1 piece into a 6x9-inch rectangle on a lightly floured surface.

🍃 Sprinkle the dough lightly with the herb mixture. Roll up the dough from a long side; tuck the ends under.

🍃 Place the loaf in a 4x8-inch or 4x9-inch loaf pan lightly coated with nonstick cooking spray.

🍃 Repeat with the remaining 2 pieces of dough. Let rise in a warm place for 4 to 8 hours or until doubled in bulk.

🍃 Bake at 350 degrees for 25 to 35 minutes or until golden brown. Remove the loaves from the pans and cool on a wire rack.

🍃 For a soft crust, brush the tops of the hot loaves with vegetable oil or melted butter.

# POTATO BREAD WITH CARAWAY SEEDS

*Yield: 1 large loaf*

3 medium potatoes, or enough for
    1 cup mashed potatoes
1 envelope dry yeast
2½ cups warm (110 to 115 degrees)
    water, divided
8 cups (about) flour, divided
1½ tablespoons salt
½ tablespoon caraway seeds

☞ Scrub the potatoes. Boil the potatoes in water to cover in a saucepan until tender; drain. Peel the potatoes and mash well. Let cool.

☞ Dissolve the yeast in ½ cup of the water. Combine with 3 tablespoons of the flour in a large bowl and mix well. Let rise for 30 minutes.

☞ Add the remaining 2 cups warm water, salt and caraway seeds. Add the remaining flour and mashed potatoes and mix well.

☞ Turn onto a floured board. Knead for 12 to 15 minutes or until the dough is smooth and elastic. Shape into a ball. Place the dough in an oiled bowl, turning to coat the surface of the dough. Let rise in a warm draft-free place for 1 to 2 hours or until doubled in bulk.

☞ Remove the dough from the bowl. Punch the dough down. Knead on a lightly floured surface for 4 to 5 minutes or until smooth. Shape into a large round loaf. Place in a buttered 12-inch ovenproof skillet with rounded sides. Let rise for 30 to 35 minutes or until the dough is slightly above the rim of the skillet.

☞ Brush the loaf with a small amount of water. Cut a deep cross-shaped incision in the center of the loaf. Bake at 400 degrees for 1 hour to 1 hour and 15 minutes or until golden brown.

☞

*Note: If you find the dough is not quite soft enough, try letting it rise in a free-form shape on a baking sheet sprinkled with cornmeal.*

☞

# MASHED POTATO BREAD

From Ore-Ida Foods, Inc.

*Yield: 1 (1¹/₂-pound) bread machine loaf*

*2¹/₄ teaspoons dry yeast
(not rapid-rise)*
*3 cups bread flour*
*1 cup firmly packed Ore-Ida Frozen
Mashed Potatoes, thawed*
*2 tablespoons sugar*
*1¹/₂ teaspoons salt*
*2 tablespoons butter*
*³/₄ cup lukewarm (85 degrees) milk*
*¹/₄ cup lukewarm (85 degrees) water*
*2 tablespoons chopped fresh parsley
(optional)*

☙ Place the yeast, flour, potatoes, sugar, salt, butter, milk, water and parsley in the order listed in the bread machine container. If the bread machine specifies liquids first, use in the order of parsley, water, milk, butter, salt, sugar, potatoes, flour and yeast.
☙ Bake using the manufacturer's directions.

☙

*Note: If the batter is too stiff for your bread machine, add about 2 tablespoons warm water to keep it kneading.*
☙

# Sweet Potato Pone

*Yield: 6 servings*

1 pound sweet potatoes
$^1/_4$ cup melted butter
$^1/_3$ cup packed brown sugar
$^1/_3$ cup maple syrup or corn syrup
$^1/_3$ cup milk
2 eggs
$^1/_2$ teaspoon allspice
$^1/_2$ teaspoon cinnamon
$^1/_4$ teaspoon cloves
$^1/_4$ teaspoon ginger
$^1/_2$ cup chopped nuts

🖎 Wash the sweet potatoes and pierce with a fork. Bake at 350 degrees for 1 hour or until tender. Let cool.

🖎 Peel the sweet potatoes and cut each into 4 pieces. Mash in a bowl until smooth; there should be about 1 cup.

🖎 Stir the butter into the sweet potatoes. Add the brown sugar, maple syrup and milk and beat until smooth.

🖎 Beat the eggs until well mixed. Stir into the sweet potato mixture. Stir in the allspice, cinnamon, cloves and ginger. Add the nuts and mix well.

🖎 Spread the mixture in a greased 9x9-inch baking pan or 9-inch round baking pan. Bake at 350 degrees for 1 hour or until a knife inserted near the center comes out clean.

🖎 Serve warm or cold with whipped cream or ice cream.

## Idaho Notes

Since 1948, the motto

on the Idaho license

plate has been

"Famous Potatoes."

## POTATO ROSEMARY ROLLS

For a 1¹/₂-pound bread machine

*Yield: 12 rolls*

*1 cup plus 2 tablespoons warm*
*(70 to 80 degrees) water*
*2 tablespoons olive oil*
*2 tablespoons nonfat dry milk*
*¹/₂ cup instant potato flakes*
*1 tablespoon sugar*
*1 teaspoon dried rosemary*
*1 teaspoon salt*
*3 cups (or more) bread flour*
*1¹/₂ teaspoons yeast*
*1 egg, slightly beaten*
*Sesame seeds or poppy seeds to taste*
*Crushed rosemary to taste*

🥐 Measure the water, olive oil, dry milk powder, potato flakes, sugar, dried rosemary, salt, bread flour and yeast into the bread machine container. Process in the dough/manual cycle using the manufacturer's directions.

🥐 Remove the dough from the pan. Knead in additional bread flour if needed to make the dough easy to handle.

🥐 Divide the dough into 12 pieces. Roll each into a 10-inch rope, tucking under the end. Place 2 inches apart on a greased large baking sheet. Let rise, covered, for 45 minutes or until doubled in bulk.

🥐 Brush the tops with the egg. Sprinkle with the sesame seeds and crushed rosemary.

🥐 Bake at 375 degrees for 15 to 20 minutes or until golden brown.

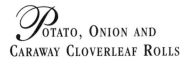

# POTATO, ONION AND CARAWAY CLOVERLEAF ROLLS

*Yield: 16 rolls*

*¹/₄ cup unsalted butter, at room
    temperature, divided*
*1¹/₂ cups chopped onions*
*1 tablespoon caraway seeds*
*1 (10-ounce) russet potato*
*³/₄ cup warm (110 to 115 degrees)
    water, divided*
*2 envelopes dry yeast*
*¹/₄ teaspoon plus ¹/₃ cup sugar,
    divided*
*2¹/₂ teaspoons salt*
*3 large eggs*
*3¹/₄ cups (or more) bread flour*

🍂 Melt 1 tablespoon of the butter in a large skillet. Add the onions. Sauté for 12 minutes or until golden brown. Add the caraway seeds. Sauté for 3 minutes. Remove from the heat and let cool.

🍂 Pierce the potato with a fork. Microwave on High for 9 minutes or until very tender, turning once. Peel the potato and mash until very smooth. Place ¹/₂ cup of the mashed potato in a large mixer bowl. Reserve the remainder of the mashed potato for another use.

🍂 Mix ¹/₂ cup of the water, yeast and ¹/₄ teaspoon of the sugar in a glass measure. Let stand for 10 minutes or until the yeast is dissolved and the mixture is slightly foamy.

🍂 Add the salt, remaining 3 tablespoons butter and ¹/₃ cup sugar to the mashed potato in the mixer bowl. Beat until smooth. Add the remaining ¹/₄ cup water and 2 eggs, beating until blended. Add the yeast mixture and mix until blended. Stir in the onion mixture. Add 3 cups of the flour 1 cup at a time. Beat for 4 minutes or until the dough is smooth but slightly sticky.

🍂 Turn onto a floured surface. Knead for 5 minutes or until smooth and elastic, adding the remaining flour if needed. Shape into a ball. Place in a greased bowl, turning to coat the surface of the dough. Cover with plastic wrap and then a towel. Let rise in a warm draft-free area for 1 hour or until doubled in bulk.

🍂 Grease 2 baking sheets. Punch the dough down. Turn onto a floured surface. Knead for 2 minutes. Divide into 16 equal portions. Divide each portion into 3 equal pieces. Roll each piece firmly into a smooth ball. For each roll, arrange 3 balls on a baking sheet so that the balls touch at the center. Cover with clean kitchen towels. Let rise in a warm draft-free area for 45 minutes or until puffy and almost doubled in bulk.

🍂 Position 1 oven rack in the center and 1 rack in the top third of the oven. Beat the remaining egg and brush over the rolls. Bake at 375 degrees for 20 minutes or until the rolls are golden brown and sound hollow when tapped, switching the baking sheets halfway through the baking time.

# POTATO CRESCENT ROLLS

*Yield: 18 to 20 rolls*

*¹/₂ cup sugar*
*¹/₂ cup warm (110 to 115 degrees) water*
*1 envelope dry yeast*
*¹/₄ cup butter, softened*
*1 cup unseasoned cooled mashed potatoes*
*3 eggs, divided*
*1 teaspoon salt*
*3 to 4 cups flour*
*1 tablespoon cold water*
*Sesame seeds or poppy seeds*

🐟 Dissolve the sugar in the warm water in a small bowl. Stir in the yeast.

🐟 Cream the butter in a large mixer bowl. Beat in the potatoes, 2 eggs and salt. Add the yeast mixture and mix well.

🐟 Add 3 cups of the flour gradually, beating well after each addition. Turn onto a floured surface. Knead until the dough is smooth and elastic, adding the remaining flour if needed. Let stand, covered with a towel, for 10 minutes.

🐟 Roll the dough into a ¹/₄-inch-thick rectangle on a floured board. Cut into 5x5x6-inch triangles. Lightly oil 2 baking sheets or spray with nonstick cooking spray. Starting from the long side, roll the triangles into crescent shapes similar to croissants. Place at least 4 inches apart on the baking sheets, keeping the middle points down. Let rise, covered with a towel, for 1¹/₂ to 2 hours or until almost doubled in bulk.

🐟 Beat the remaining egg with the cold water in a bowl. Brush over the top of the rolls, taking care that no egg wash drops onto the baking sheets. Sprinkle with sesame seeds.

🐟 Bake for 10 to 15 minutes or until browned.

 STICKY POTATO BUNS

*Yield: 24 buns*

## Dough

*2 medium potatoes, peeled,*
   *cut into quarters*
*3 cups water*
*¹/₂ cup sugar*
*¹/₂ cup butter*
*1¹/₂ teaspoons salt*
*2 eggs*
*1 envelope dry yeast*
*7 cups (about) flour*

## Topping

*1 cup butter*
*2 cups packed brown sugar*
*1¹/₂ teaspoons cinnamon*
*¹/₂ cup dark corn syrup*
*3 cups chopped pecans or walnuts*

## Filling

*¹/₄ cup melted butter*
*¹/₂ cup sugar*
*2 teaspoons cinnamon*

🖝 For the dough, boil the potatoes in the water in a saucepan. Drain, reserving 1¹/₂ cups cooking liquid. Mash the potatoes well. Combine with the sugar, butter and salt and mix well. Cool to lukewarm. Add the reserved cooking liquid, eggs and yeast and beat until thoroughly mixed. Stir in enough of the flour to make a stiff dough.

🖝 Turn the dough onto a floured surface. Knead for 8 to 10 minutes or until smooth and elastic. Place the dough in a large oiled bowl, turning to grease the surface. Let stand in a warm place, covered with plastic wrap, for 1¹/₂ hours or until doubled in bulk.

🖝 For the topping, boil the butter, brown sugar, cinnamon and corn syrup in a saucepan for 1 minute. Sprinkle the pecans into a generously buttered baking pan or three 8-inch round baking pans. Pour the brown sugar mixture over the pecans.

🖝 Punch the dough down and divide into halves. Roll each half into a 10x16-inch rectangle on a lightly floured surface.

🖝 For the filling, spread 1¹/₂ table-spoons of the melted butter over each rectangle. Sprinkle each with a mixture of the sugar and cinnamon.

🖝 Roll the dough up as for a jelly roll, starting with the longest edge. Cut into 1¹/₂-inch slices. Arrange over the topping in the pan. Brush with the remaining 1 tablespoon butter. Let stand in a warm place for 30 minutes or until doubled in bulk.

🖝 Bake at 350 degrees for 30 to 35 minutes or until golden brown.

🖝 Invert immediately onto a serving plate. Serve warm.

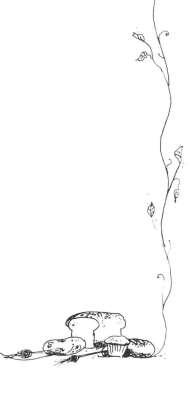

# RAISED POTATO BISCUITS

*Yield: 5 to 6 dozen*

*6 cups flour, sifted*
*¹/₂ cup sugar*
*1 teaspoon baking powder*
*¹/₂ teaspoon baking soda*
*1 teaspoon salt*
*¹/₂ cup mashed russet potatoes*
*¹/₂ cup shortening*
*2 cups scalded milk*
*1 envelope dry yeast*
*¹/₂ cup lukewarm water*
*Butter*

☞ Sift the flour, sugar, baking powder, baking soda and salt together. Set aside.

☞ Combine the potatoes and shortening in a large bowl. Pour the milk over the potato mixture, stirring until the shortening is melted. Let stand until cool.

☞ Dissolve the yeast in the water in a small bowl. Add to the cooled potato mixture. Add the flour mixture gradually, stirring until a soft dough forms. Let rise, covered, in a warm place until doubled in bulk.

☞ Grease baking sheets or shallow baking pans.

☞ Stir down the dough. Turn onto a lightly floured surface, working with half the dough at a time if desired. Roll out as for biscuits. Cut with a biscuit cutter. Brush with butter. Leave in the shape of biscuits or fold over as for pocketbook rolls. Place on the prepared baking sheets. Let rise, covered, in a warm place until almost doubled in bulk.

☞ Bake at 450 to 475 degrees for several minutes or just until set but not browned. Remove from the oven and let cool. Wrap well and freeze until needed.

☞ Brush the prebaked biscuits with butter. Bake at 450 to 475 degrees for 5 to 6 minutes or until golden brown.

# Mashed Potato Biscuits

*Yield: 18 biscuits*

1 large russet potato, peeled, cut
    into chunks
2 large cloves of garlic,
    finely chopped
3/4 teaspoon salt, divided
3 tablespoons butter, divided
1 cup flour
1 tablespoon baking powder
1/2 teaspoon sugar
3 tablespoons chilled shortening
2/3 cup sour cream
3 tablespoons snipped chives or
    chopped green onions
3 tablespoons milk

🐟 Combine the potato, garlic and
1/4 teaspoon of the salt with water to
cover in a saucepan. Bring to a boil
over high heat; reduce the heat to low.
Cook, covered, for 20 minutes or until
tender; drain. Mash the potato with
1 tablespoon of the butter.

🐟 Mix the flour, baking powder,
remaining 1/2 teaspoon salt and sugar
in a large bowl. Cut in the potato,
shortening and remaining 2 tablespoons butter with a pastry blender or
2 knives until crumbly. Add the sour
cream and chives, stirring until a
dough forms.

🐟 Turn onto a floured surface. Roll
3/4 inch thick with a floured rolling
pin. Cut out with a 2-inch round or
decorative biscuit cutter. Gather the
dough trimmings and reroll. Cut out
additional biscuits. Continue until all
the dough is used. Brush the biscuits
with the milk.

🐟 Place the biscuits 1 inch apart on
a greased and lightly floured baking
sheet. Bake at 450 degrees for 12 to
15 minutes. Remove to a wire rack to
cool slightly.

🐟

*Note: Mashed sweet potatoes
would make a tasty alternative
to white potatoes in this recipe.
If using sweet potatoes, omit the
chives and stir in 3 tablespoons
chopped pecans.*

🐟

Because of unusual farming obstacles, many Idaho farmers seek answers to their problems from the University of Idaho's Agricultural Experiment Stations. The scientists answer the farmers' potato questions on such topics as seed-piece size, irrigation, and storage. The scientists then pass along their findings to the farmers, enabling farming and irrigation practices to improve.

# LEFSE

*Yield: 15 lefse*

*6 cups russet potatoes, peeled, cut*
*into quarters*
*2 teaspoons salt, divided*
*3 tablespoons butter*
*½ cup milk*
*1 cup flour*
*1 teaspoon baking powder*
*1 tablespoon sugar*

🖙 Combine the potatoes, 1 teaspoon of the salt and water to cover in a large saucepan. Cook for 20 to 30 minutes or until tender; drain. Mash the potatoes with the butter and milk.
🖙 Add the flour, remaining 1 teaspoon salt, baking powder and sugar and mix together as for pastry dough.
🖙 For each lefse, roll 1 heaping tablespoon of dough extremely thin on a floured board.

🖙 Cook on a hot nonstick griddle or skillet for 1½ to 2 minutes or until 1 side is beginning to brown. Turn carefully. Cook for 45 to 60 seconds for the other side. Remove from the griddle. Fold in half and place between thin towels to cool. Wrap in plastic wrap to store in the refrigerator.

🖙

*Note: Lefse are the Norwegian equivalent to tortilla shells or pita bread and are good served with butter and jam or buttered and sprinkled with sugar. Norwegians wrap lefse around lutefisk or other fish or meat. This recipe was brought over from Norway many years ago.*

🖙

# POTATO CREPES

*Yield: 24 large crepes, or
70 cocktail-sized crepes*

*3 cups cold unseasoned
    mashed potatoes*
*2³/₄ cups milk*
*³/₄ cup flour*
*1¹/₂ teaspoons salt*
*¹/₄ teaspoon white pepper*
*4 eggs*
*Clarified butter (see Note)*

🖙 Combine the potatoes, milk, flour, salt and pepper in a mixer bowl and mix well. Beat in the eggs 1 at a time. Chill for 2 hours.

🖙 For cocktail-sized crepes, cook dollar-sized pancakes on a hot griddle brushed with clarified butter.

🖙 For larger crepes, brush a nonstick or well-seasoned 10-inch skillet with clarified butter. Heat over medium heat until a small amount of batter browns on 1 side in 1 minute.

🖙 Pour in 3 tablespoons of the batter. Rotate the skillet until the batter forms a thin 6-inch-round pancake. Cook until browned on 1 side. Turn carefully. Cook for 30 seconds. Turn out on paper towels.

🖙 Repeat with the remaining batter, brushing the skillet with clarified butter between every 2 to 3 pancakes.

🖙

*Note: For clarified butter, melt unsalted butter slowly to evaporate most of the water. Skim any foam from the top. Then pour off the clear butter, leaving behind the milky residue. This clear (clarified) butter is great for frying because it has a higher smoking point.*

🖙

# RASPBERRY ALMOND MUFFINS

*Yield: 12 muffins*

*¹/₂ cup rolled oats*
*¹/₄ cup slivered almonds*
*2 cups flour*
*¹/₂ cup sugar*
*1 tablespoon baking powder*
*¹/₄ teaspoon salt*
*1 egg*
*³/₄ cup skim milk*
*¹/₄ cup vegetable oil*
*¹/₂ teaspoon almond extract*
*¹/₂ cup mashed potatoes*
*¹/₂ pint fresh or frozen raspberries*

🖜 Toast the oats in a skillet over medium heat until lightly browned. Set aside.

🖜 Spread the almonds on a foil-lined baking sheet. Toast at 350 degrees for 5 minutes or until golden brown and fragrant.

🖜 Mix the flour, sugar, baking powder and salt in a large bowl.

🖜 Beat the egg, skim milk, oil and flavoring in a small bowl until blended. Stir in the mashed potatoes.

🖜 Add the potato mixture to the flour mixture, stirring just until moistened. Fold in the raspberries and toasted oats.

🖜 Spoon the batter into 12 paper-lined muffin cups. Top with the toasted almonds.

🖜 Bake at 400 degrees for 20 minutes.

 ## BLUEBERRY PUMPKIN POTATO MUFFINS

*Yield: 12 muffins*

### Batter

*1²/₃ cups plus 1 tablespoon flour, divided*
*1 teaspoon baking soda*
*¹/₂ teaspoon baking powder*
*¹/₂ teaspoon salt*
*1 teaspoon cinnamon*
*¹/₄ teaspoon nutmeg*
*¹/₂ cup solid-pack canned pumpkin*
*¹/₂ cup mashed potatoes*
*¹/₄ cup evaporated milk*
*¹/₃ cup shortening*
*1 cup packed brown sugar*
*1 egg*
*1 cup fresh or frozen blueberries*

### Streusel

*2 tablespoons flour*
*2 tablespoons sugar*
*¹/₄ teaspoon cinnamon*
*1 tablespoon butter, softened*

🖝 For the batter, combine 1²/₃ cups of the flour, baking soda, baking powder, salt, cinnamon and nutmeg in a large bowl and mix well.

🖝 Blend the pumpkin, mashed potatoes and evaporated milk in a medium bowl.

🖝 Cream the shortening and brown sugar in a mixer bowl. Add the egg, beating until the mixture is light and fluffy. Add the flour mixture and pumpkin mixture alternately, beating well after each addition.

🖝 Toss the blueberries with the remaining 1 tablespoon flour. Stir gently into the batter.

🖝 For the streusel, combine the flour, sugar, cinnamon and butter in a bowl and mix until crumbly.

🖝 Fill 12 paper-lined muffin cups with the batter. Sprinkle with the streusel.

🖝 Bake at 350 degrees for 40 minutes or until a wooden pick inserted in the center comes out clean.

# CINNAMON ROLLS

*Yield: 20 to 24 rolls*

## Dough
*1 envelope dry yeast*
*1¹/₂ cups warm water*
*1 cup mashed potatoes*
*²/₃ cup sugar*
*²/₃ cup shortening*
*2 eggs*
*1¹/₂ teaspoons salt*
*6 to 7 cups flour*

## Sauce
*2¹/₄ cups packed brown sugar*
*1 cup butter, softened*
*¹/₄ cup sour cream*
*Cinnamon (optional)*
*Chopped nuts (optional)*

🖙 For the dough, dissolve the yeast in the warm water. Let stand in a warm place for 10 minutes or until bubbly. Stir in the potatoes, sugar, shortening, eggs and salt.

🖙 Add 3 cups of the flour and mix well. Add enough of the remaining flour to make a soft dough. Knead until smooth and elastic. Let rise, covered, for 4 hours or until doubled in bulk.

🖙 For the sauce, combine the brown sugar, butter, sour cream and cinnamon in a bowl, mixing until smooth. Stir in the nuts. Set aside.

🖙 Punch the dough down. Roll into a ¹/₂-inch-thick rectangle on a lightly floured surface. Spread half the sauce over the dough. Spread the remaining sauce in a 9x13-inch baking dish. Roll the dough as for a jelly roll, starting with a long side. Cut into 1¹/₂-inch slices.

🖙 Place the rolls in the prepared baking dish. Let rise, covered, for 2 hours or until doubled in bulk.

🖙 Bake at 400 degrees for 15 minutes. Reduce the oven temperature to 350 degrees. Bake for 30 to 40 minutes longer or until golden brown.

🖙 Let cool in the baking dish for 10 minutes. Invert the rolls onto a serving platter.

# CINNAMON COFFEE CAKE

*Yield: 2 loaves*

## Dough

4 to 4¹/₂ cups flour, divided
2 envelopes dry yeast
¹/₂ cup water
¹/₂ cup sugar
¹/₂ cup butter
¹/₂ teaspoon salt
2 eggs
¹/₂ cup mashed potatoes or prepared
    instant mashed potatoes
¹/₂ cup packed brown sugar
2 teaspoons ground cinnamon
¹/₂ cup melted butter

## Icing (optional)

1 egg white
¹/₈ teaspoon salt
1 to 1¹/₂ cups confectioners' sugar
¹/₂ teaspoon vanilla extract

🌿 For the dough, mix 2 cups of the flour with the yeast in a mixer bowl.

🌿 Combine the water, sugar, butter and salt in a saucepan. Heat over low heat until warm (105 to 115 degrees), stirring occasionally. Add to the flour mixture. Beat at medium speed for 2 minutes or until smooth.

🌿 Blend in the eggs and mashed potatoes. Add 1 cup of the flour. Beat at medium speed for 1 minute. Add enough of the remaining flour to make a moderately stiff dough.

🌿 Turn the dough onto a lightly floured surface. Knead for 8 to 10 minutes or until smooth and elastic. Shape into a ball. Place in a lightly buttered bowl, turning to grease the surface. Let rise, covered, in a warm draft-free place for 1¹/₂ hours or until doubled in bulk.

🌿 Punch the dough down and divide into halves. Let rest for 10 minutes. Shape the dough into loaves. Place in buttered 5x9-inch loaf pans.

🌿 Sprinkle the loaves with a mixture of the brown sugar and cinnamon. Drizzle with the melted butter. Let rise in a warm place for 1 hour or until doubled in bulk.

🌿 Bake at 350 degrees for 30 to 35 minutes or until the loaves test done. Cool in the pans for 5 minutes.

🌿 For the icing, beat the egg white with the salt in a mixer bowl until soft peaks form. Fold in the confectioners' sugar, beating constantly until of spreading consistency. Beat in the vanilla. Drizzle over the warm coffee cake.

# Soups

## EVIL ANNE AND THE MUSTARD SEED

I grew up on a potato farm outside Wendell, Idaho. My favorite fall dinner included creamy potato soup, fresh-baked corn bread, apple salad, and gingerbread cookies. My mother's potato soup was a meal in itself. She used fresh cream, sweet onions, and meaty potatoes. My favorite part was the mustard seeds. I loved the feel in my mouth of tender potato chunks, smooth cream, and crunchy mustard seeds.

My mother put mustard seeds in just about everything. Soups, stews, gravies, stuffing; it all had to have mustard seeds. My mother was a faithful believer, and one of her favorite Biblical scriptures guaranteed that if your faith is only the size of a mustard seed, you can move mountains. I knew that to be true.

The mustard seed promise came in handy the autumn of my twelfth year. My best friends and I had planned our "last" trick-or-treating venture for Halloween. It was our last because, after all, we were almost grown up and only little kids went trick-or-treating. We met a few days before Halloween to devise our plans. One girl dared us to visit Evil Anne, the mysterious old woman who lived in a haunted mansion just outside of town. Amid nervous giggles, horrified refusals, and proud boasting, it was decided that a dozen of us would take the challenge.

The legend was that Evil Anne only came out at Halloween to capture and eat little children. She was a huge woman with frantic black hair, evil black eyes, and a shrill scream that could be heard clear into town. Everyone knew that she had married her wealthy husband many years earlier just to get his extensive farm properties. He had disappeared shortly after the marriage, and rumor had it that she had thrown him into the lagoon behind the pig barn.

That Halloween, the twelve of us dressed in our homemade costumes as ghosts, pirates, cowboys, and bums using old sheets, baggy coats, and whatever we could sneak from siblings and parents. I was a clown and wore my dad's shoes, baggy pants, a frizzy wig, and a huge red nose.

A cool breeze provided the perfect atmosphere as we set out at dusk toward Evil Anne's neglected mansion. As we approached the gloomy property, our eager anticipation began to sink. We climbed upon the rotting fence and peered beyond the tangle of weeds, vines, and old leaves. The house, once a glorious masterpiece of construction, loomed as a monster of decay. Bare wood cried for paint, the front porch sagged in the middle, and

a torn curtain waved from a broken top window as if calling for help. A single light shown faintly from the dirty front window.

We pushed open the rusted gate and tiptoed through the weeds and sticks. The silence was intense, and I could feel my heart beating beneath my baggy clothes. The wind whistled through the naked trees and scattered the trash around the door. Even the full moon was afraid to come all the way out and sought shelter behind some heavy clouds.

Two of our friends wanted to leave. The rest were too afraid to say anything. Finally, I stepped ahead to knock on the door. In my mind, I kept remembering the mustard seed. *All I needed was faith, and I could move this mountain.* Yes, I could walk right up to Evil Anne and holler "trick or treat!"

As I stepped on the porch, it groaned under my weight. My trembling hand reached tentatively and knocked three times on the old door. We all held our breath. Suddenly we jumped and screamed as we heard the growl of an angry dog inside the house. My friends turned and ran to the country road but I was too scared to move. My eyes stared as the knob turned and the door squeaked open. There, in all her glory, stood Evil Anne!

A mountain of a woman, she towered over me, much grander than my own vivid imagination. She wore what looked like a poncho made from a soiled red blanket. Her hair was wild and frizzy, clumping over her shoulders almost to her waist. If there was a waist. Her face was round, white, and looked like a raw pie with two beady eyes at the top. She made a guttural sound as she breathed, and her ample bosom rose and fell like an inflated raft on a rolling sea.

"Shut up!" she snapped at the growling mutt. The animal instantly obeyed. Then she focused on me and whispered through cracked lips. "What do you want?"

"Trick or Treat?" I could barely hear my own voice. I held out my sack, more like a meager offering than an eager request. *Remember the mustard seed, I thought. The mustard seed.*

Then Evil Anne laughed. Her head went back and she heaved a contorted, raspy sound that was more like forcing old air from leather bellows. The musty breath from the deep laugh exploded from her gaping mouth, rippled her numerous chins, and hit me in the face. I felt my clown nose quivering. Then she turned and reached into a cracked pottery bowl perched on a disheveled stack of old *House Beautiful* magazines. She pulled out a small object and threw it in my sack. For a second, our eyes met. I suspected then that I would end up in her stew pot. But she just grinned and showed what teeth still remained. "Happy Halloween," she muttered, then turned and slammed the door.

I slapped my big shoes back to the others and we ran all the way back to town before we stopped to catch our breath. They all crowded around me to see what was in my sack. I slowly retrieved an old keychain that had a small plastic potato dangling from a ring. Attached was a yellow note that read: A gift for you from Anne Service, Miss Weiser County, 1920.

We laughed at the prize and at ourselves. Evil Anne was just a lonely former beauty queen! I put the prize in my pocket and we headed off to mooch from the safer homes in town. Later, my mom took us home for potato soup, corn bread, and popcorn balls.

Back in the safety of my home, I decided that someday I would take some potato soup with lots of mustard seeds to the old woman. But, I'd do it in the daylight.

— *by Elaine Ambrose*

# POTATO SOUP

This is the recipe for the soup mentioned in Elaine Ambrose's story of Evil Anne and the mustard seed, page 65.

*Yield: 8 servings*

*1 pound bacon or bulk sausage*
*1 cup chopped onion*
*1 cup chopped celery*
*4 large russet potatoes,*
*    peeled, cubed*
*1 tablespoon mustard seeds*
*2 teaspoons salt*
*1 cup light cream*
*2 cups milk*
*2 (10¹/₂ ounces each) cans any*
*    flavor cream soup (optional)*

## Garnish
*Chopped parsley*

🕊 Cook the bacon in a saucepan over low heat until crisp. Remove to a warm plate with a slotted spoon and drain the saucepan, reserving 1 tablespoon drippings.

🕊 Add the onion and celery to the reserved drippings in the saucepan and sauté until tender. Add the potatoes, mustard seeds and salt. Add just enough water to cover the potatoes.

🕊 Simmer for 15 minutes or until the potatoes are tender but still firm; reduce the heat. Stir in the cream and milk. Add the canned soup if a thicker soup is desired. Cook just until heated through; do not boil.

🕊 Pour into large mugs and top with the crumbled bacon. Garnish with parsley.

🕊 Add corn bread, apple salad, gingerbread cookies and cider for a complete autumn supper. Then find a cozy blanket and a good book.

# BASQUE POTATO CHORIZO STEW

*Yield: 6 to 8 servings*

2 tablespoons olive oil
1 medium leek, chopped
  (about 2¹/₃ cups)
4 (3 ounces each) chorizo sausages,
  cut into ¹/₄-inch pieces
3³/₄ pounds peeled or unpeeled
  russet potatoes, cut into
  1-inch pieces
1 tablespoon hot or sweet paprika
1 tablespoon salt
4 cups water

☞ Heat the olive oil in a saucepan over medium heat. Add the leek and cook until translucent, stirring frequently; reduce the heat if necessary to prevent overbrowning.

☞ Add the sausage. Cook for 5 minutes. Stir in the potatoes, paprika, salt and water. Bring to a boil over high heat and reduce the heat.

☞ Simmer, partially covered, for 30 minutes or until the potatoes are tender; remove the cover. Increase the heat and bring to a boil.

☞ Mash some of the potatoes with a fork or potato masher. Adjust the salt.

☞ Ladle into soup bowls and serve with a hearty bread.

☞

*Note: If chorizo is not available, substitute another spicy sausage such as linguiça.*

☞

## IDAHO NOTES

Idaho's state flower

is the Syringa.

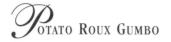

# Potato Roux Gumbo

*Yield: 6 to 8 servings*

*1/4 cup vegetable oil*
*1 cup instant potato flakes*
*1/2 cup chopped green bell pepper*
*1 cup chopped onion*
*1 cup chopped celery*
*2 cloves of garlic, minced*
*1/4 cup chopped fresh parsley, or*
  *2 tablespoons dried parsley*
*6 cups water*
*3 boneless skinless chicken breast*
  *halves (about 1 1/2 pounds)*
*1/2 pound smoked sausage, sliced*
*2 dashes of Tabasco sauce, or*
  *to taste*
*1 teaspoon salt*
*1/2 teaspoon pepper*
*4 cups cooked rice*
*Gumbo filé powder to taste*
  *(optional)*

## Garnish
*Parsley sprigs*

☛ Heat the oil in a large heavy saucepan over medium heat. Stir in the potato flakes. Cook until the color of bread crust, stirring constantly.

☛ Add the green pepper, onion, celery, garlic and parsley. Sauté until tender and translucent. Add the water and increase the heat to high. Bring to a boil.

☛ Add the chicken and sausage to the saucepan. Bring to a boil and reduce the heat. Stir in the Tabasco sauce, salt and pepper.

☛ Simmer, loosely covered, for 1 hour, stirring occasionally. Remove and shred the chicken; return to the soup.

☛ Place 2/3 to 1/2 cup rice in each soup bowl. Ladle the soup over the rice. Sprinkle with the filé and mix well. Let stand for 5 minutes.

☛ Garnish with a sprig of parsley and serve with a fruit salad.

☛ Filé powder is available in the spice section of most grocery stores. It serves as both a flavoring and thickening agent. Soup does not reheat well after the filé has been added, so it should be added just before serving.

☛

*Note: You can reduce the fat in the sausage by boiling it before adding it to the soup. Substitute any combination of meat or seafood that you prefer.*

☛

#  Sopa de Albóndigas

*Yield: 6 to 8 servings*

## Meatballs

*1 pound ground beef*
*1 egg*
*2 tablespoons uncooked long grain*
*white rice*
*1 tablespoon Worcestershire sauce*
*¼ teaspoon garlic powder*
*¼ teaspoon oregano*
*1 teaspoon salt*
*½ teaspoon pepper*

## Soup

*¾ cup chopped onion*
*½ cup sliced celery*
*2 carrots, sliced (about 1 cup)*
*1 cup frozen corn or*
*mixed vegetables*
*2 potatoes, cubed (about 1½ cups)*
*2 tablespoons uncooked long grain*
*white rice*
*1 (8-ounce) can tomato sauce*
*¼ teaspoon oregano*
*1 teaspoon chili powder*
*5 beef bouillon cubes*
*6 cups water*

## Garnish

*Sour cream*
*Tortilla chips*

🖝 For the meatballs, combine the ground beef, egg, rice, Worcestershire sauce, garlic powder, oregano, salt and pepper in a bowl and mix well. Shape into 1-inch balls.

🖝 Drop the meatballs into a saucepan of boiling water. Cook for 10 to 15 minutes or until cooked through; drain.

🖝 For the soup, combine the onion, celery, carrots, corn, potatoes, rice, tomato sauce, oregano, chili powder, bouillon cubes and water in a large saucepan. Bring to a boil and reduce the heat.

🖝 Simmer for several minutes. Add the meatballs. Simmer for 30 minutes or until the vegetables are tender.

🖝 Ladle into soup bowls and garnish with sour cream and tortilla chips.

🖝

*This is a tasty change-of-pace soup with a Spanish and Mexican heritage.*

🖝

## Potato Trivia

In 1974, an Englishman named Eric Jenkins grew 370 pounds of potatoes from one plant.

# ITALIAN SAUSAGE AND GARBANZO BEAN SOUP

*Yield: 4 servings*

1 (16-ounce) package dried
    garbanzos (chick-peas)
10 cups water
1 cup chopped celery
1 cup chopped onion
1 large ham hock
1 teaspoon salt
$^1/_2$ teaspoon pepper
2 cups diced potatoes
8 ounces pepperoni, sliced
8 ounces Italian sausage and/or
    kielbasa sausage, sliced
3 cloves of garlic, crushed

## Garnish
*Grated Parmesan cheese*

🖙 Rinse and sort the garbanzos.
Combine with water to cover in a
saucepan. Let stand for 8 hours or
longer; drain.

🖙 Combine the soaked beans with
10 cups water in a large saucepan.
Bring to a boil and turn off the heat.
Let stand for 1 hour.

🖙 Add the celery, onion, ham hock,
salt and pepper. Simmer, covered, for
5 to 6 hours or until the beans are
tender but still firm; do not overcook.

🖙 Add the potatoes, pepperoni,
sausages and garlic. Simmer for
1 hour longer. Adjust the seasonings
to taste.

🖙 Ladle into soup bowls and garnish
with Parmesan cheese. Serve with
French bread.

# Hearty Stew

*Yield: 6 to 8 servings*

2 tablespoons vegetable oil
2 pounds stew beef, cut into
    1-inch cubes
2 onions, chopped
1 (24-ounce) can tomatoes, crushed
1 (14-ounce) can beef broth
1 ($10^1/_2$-ounce) can golden
    mushroom soup
1 ($10^1/_2$-ounce) can water
1 bay leaf
1 teaspoon marjoram
1 teaspoon garlic powder
1 teaspoon basil
2 teaspoons salt
1 teaspoon pepper
2 cups diced potatoes
1 cup sliced carrots
1 cup sliced mushrooms
$^1/_2$ cup sliced celery
$^1/_2$ cup frozen peas

☞ Heat the oil in a heavy saucepan. Add the stew beef and onions and cook until browned. Add the tomatoes, broth, soup, water, bay leaf, marjoram, garlic powder, basil, salt and pepper. Simmer for 45 minutes.

☞ Add the potatoes and carrots. Cook over low heat for 30 minutes. Stir in the mushrooms and celery. Simmer for 15 minutes.

☞ Stir in the peas. Cook just until heated through. Discard the bay leaf.

☞ Ladle into soup bowls and serve with bread and crisp apple slices.

# SPICY FISH SOUP

*Yield: 6 servings*

2 onions, chopped
2 carrots, peeled, chopped
1 green bell pepper, chopped
1 red bell pepper, chopped
2 or 3 cloves of garlic,
    finely chopped
1 tablespoon olive oil
1 (28-ounce) can whole
    peeled tomatoes
3 ($^1$/$_2$x3 inches each) strips of
    orange peel
$^1$/$_2$ teaspoon fennel seeds
$^1$/$_2$ teaspoon thyme
$^1$/$_2$ teaspoon dried red pepper flakes,
    crushed
1 bay leaf
3 medium potatoes, peeled, cut into
    $^1$/$_2$-inch cubes (about 1 pound)
3 cups water
1 cup white wine
2 pounds fresh or frozen cod,
    halibut or haddock,
    cut into chunks
$^1$/$_2$ cup minced fresh parsley
1 teaspoon salt
$^1$/$_2$ teaspoon black pepper

🐟 Sauté the onions, carrots, bell peppers and garlic in the heated olive oil in a large saucepan until tender.

🐟 Add the tomatoes, orange peel, fennel seeds, thyme, crushed pepper flakes and bay leaf. Bring to a boil.

🐟 Add the potatoes. Simmer, covered, for 15 minutes. Add the water and wine. Bring to a boil and reduce the heat. Simmer for 10 minutes.

🐟 Stir in the fish and parsley. Cook just until the fish flakes easily; do not overcook. Discard the orange peel and bay leaf. Season with the salt and black pepper.

🐟 Ladle into soup bowls and serve with bread and green salad.

# ERBED POTATO AND FISH SOUP

*Yield: 2 servings*

*1¹/₂ medium leeks*
*2 tablespoons melted butter*
*8 ounces red potatoes, peeled,*
  *cut into ¹/₂-inch pieces*
*2 cups bottled clam juice*
*2 tablespoons chopped fresh thyme,*
  *or 2 teaspoons dried thyme*
*8 ounces firm fish fillets such as*
  *haddock, halibut or cod*
*³/₄ teaspoon salt*
*¹/₈ teaspoon pepper*
*¹/₂ cup whipping cream*

## Garnish
*2 lemon slices*
*2 sprigs of thyme*

☞ Cut the white and pale green parts of the leeks only into thin slices. Cook, covered, in the butter in a large heavy saucepan over medium heat for 3 minutes or until tender, stirring occasionally. Add the potatoes. Cook for 1 minute, stirring constantly.

☞ Add the clam juice and thyme. Bring to a boil and reduce the heat. Simmer, covered, over medium-low heat for 6 minutes.

☞ Cut the fish into ¹/₂-inch pieces. Add to the saucepan. Simmer, uncovered, for 5 minutes or until the potatoes are tender and the fish flakes easily.

☞ Season with salt and pepper. Add the cream. Cook just until heated through; do not boil.

☞ Ladle into soup bowls. Garnish with lemon slices and sprigs of thyme.

☞

*Note: This delicious first-course soup served with baguettes is a great complement to a hearty beef main dish. The recipe can be easily doubled.*

☞

 CLAM CHOWDER

*Yield: 4 servings*

*2 cups chopped russet potatoes*
*1 cup minced onion*
*1 cup minced celery*
*¹/₂ cup grated carrot*
*2 (6¹/₂ ounces each) cans*
  *minced clams*
*³/₄ cup butter*
*³/₄ cup flour*
*4 cups half-and-half*
*2 or 3 drops of Tabasco sauce*
  *(optional)*
*¹/₂ teaspoon sugar*
*1¹/₂ teaspoons salt*
*¹/₄ teaspoon pepper*

## Garnish
*¹/₄ cup butter, cut into 4 slices*
*Paprika*

🖙 Combine the potatoes, onion, celery and carrot in a large saucepan.

🖙 Drain the clams, reserving the juice.

🖙 Add the clam juice to the saucepan with enough water to cover the vegetables. Simmer for 20 minutes.

🖙 Melt the butter in a medium skillet over medium-low heat. Stir in the flour. Cook until bubbly, stirring constantly. Remove from the heat and stir in the half-and-half. Cook until thickened and bubbly, stirring constantly.

🖙 Add the white sauce, clams, Tabasco sauce, sugar, salt and pepper to the vegetables in the saucepan. Simmer for 20 minutes, stirring frequently.

🖙 Ladle into soup bowls. Garnish with 1 tablespoon butter and paprika.

🖙

*This family recipe is very rich and is a great treat to serve on Christmas Eve.*

🖙

## Basque Lentil Potato Soup

This soup is best when made twenty-four hours in advance.

*Yield: 4 to 6 servings*

1 pound dried lentils
6 cups water
$^{1}/_{2}$ cup cubed potato
$^{1}/_{2}$ cup diced carrot
$^{1}/_{2}$ cup diced celery
$^{1}/_{2}$ cup diced onion
1 (8-ounce) can tomatoes, diced
3 (3 ounces each)
   chorizo sausages, diced
2 beef bouillon cubes
2 tablespoons catsup
1 tablespoon Worcestershire sauce
Salt to taste

🐭 Sort and rinse the lentils. Combine the lentils, water, potato, carrot, celery, onion, undrained tomatoes and chorizo in a large heavy saucepan. Bring to a boil and reduce the heat. Simmer for 1$^{1}/_{2}$ hours.

🐭 Add the beef bouillon, catsup and Worcestershire sauce. Simmer for 30 minutes longer. Season with salt to taste.

🐭 Serve in a bread bowl for a special treat.

🐭

*Note: If chorizo is not available, substitute another spicy sausage such as linguiça.*

🐭

### Potato Trivia

Buy only the amount of potatoes you can use in about two weeks. Store in a cool, dark place.

# FRENCH FRY POTATO
## CHEESE SOUP

*Yield: 4 to 6 servings*

1 (16-ounce) package plain frozen
   potatoes for French fries
1¹/₂ cups hot water
2 chicken bouillon cubes
2 teaspoons onion salt
¹/₈ teaspoon paprika
¹/₈ teaspoon pepper
3 cups milk (2%, 1% or skim)
1 (10¹/₂-ounce) can cream of
   celery soup
8 ounces Velveeta cheese, chopped

🌿 Combine the potatoes, water, bouillon, onion salt, paprika and pepper in a large saucepan. Bring to a boil and reduce the heat. Simmer, covered, for 8 minutes or until the potatoes are very tender.

🌿 Beat with a mixer until smooth. Add the milk and soup and mix well. Cook until heated through.

🌿 Add the cheese gradually, stirring over medium heat until melted after each addition; do not boil.

🌿 Ladle into soup bowls.

🌿

*Note: This soup recipe can be easily doubled. You may add 1 pound of browned and drained lean ground beef if desired.*

🌿

# Idaho Potato Soup with Brie

From Chef Peter Schott,
Peter Schott's New American
Cuisine Restaurant,
Boise, Idaho

*Yield: 8 servings*

## Soup

*1 leek, white part only*
*3 green onions*
*3 tablespoons unsalted butter*
*2 medium russet potatoes, cut into*
*   $^1/_4$-inch cubes*
*2 cups sliced fresh chanterelle or*
*   king bolete mushrooms*
*4 cups chicken broth*
*2 cups whipping cream*
*7 tablespoons cornstarch*
*1 cup dry sherry*
*Salt and pepper to taste*

## Croutons

*$^1/_4$ loaf baguette or French bread,*
*   sliced $^1/_4$ inch thick*
*12 ounces (60% fat) Brie cheese,*
*   sliced $^1/_4$ inch thick*

## Garnish

*2 tablespoons chopped parsley*

🍂 For the soup, cut the leek into halves lengthwise. Cut the leek and green onions into $^1/_4$-inch slices.

🍂 Heat the butter in a heavy 3- to 4-quart saucepan over medium heat until it foams. Add the leek, potatoes and mushrooms. Sauté for 5 minutes.

🍂 Add the chicken broth and bring to a boil. Stir in the cream and return to a boil; reduce the heat.

🍂 Blend the cornstarch and sherry in a cup. Stir into the simmering soup. Bring to a boil and cook for 3 minutes or until thickened, stirring constantly.

🍂 Add the green onions, salt and pepper.

🍂 For the croutons, arrange the bread slices 1 inch apart on a baking sheet. Toast in a 300-degree oven for 10 minutes or until golden brown; reduce the oven temperature to 150 degrees.

🍂 Arrange the cheese slices over the toasted bread, covering the surface completely.

🍂 Preheat 8 soup cups in the oven; remove from the oven and set the oven to broil. Ladle the soup into the cups and place 1 cheese crouton on each.

🍂 Broil 6 inches from the heat source for 30 to 45 seconds or just until the cheese melts and is light golden brown.

🍂 Garnish with the parsley and serve at once.

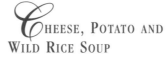

# CHEESE, POTATO AND WILD RICE SOUP

*Yield: 8 to 10 servings*

*¹/₂ cup uncooked wild rice*
*1¹/₂ cups water*
*¹/₄ cup chopped onion*
*8 ounces bacon, chopped*
*2 (10¹/₂ ounces each) cans cream of potato soup*
*¹/₂ soup can milk*
*¹/₂ soup can water*
*1 quart milk*
*2¹/₂ cups shredded American cheese or Velveeta cheese*

## Garnish
*Carrot curls*

🖝 Rinse the wild rice well. Combine with 1¹/₂ cups water in a saucepan. Bring to a boil and reduce the heat. Simmer for 45 minutes or until tender; drain and set aside.

🖝 Sauté the onion with the bacon in a skillet until the bacon is crisp; drain on a paper towel.

🖝 Combine the canned soup, ¹/₂ can milk and ¹/₂ can water in a large saucepan and mix well. Add 1 quart milk, the bacon, onion, cheese and rice. Cook until the cheese melts, stirring occasionally.

🖝 Ladle into soup bowls. Garnish with carrot curls. Serve with toasted French bread.

🖝

*Note: For more flavor, add cooked cubed potatoes.*

🖝

# Varsity Chowder

*Yield: 4 servings*

2 cups diced potatoes
2 cups boiling water
¹/₂ cup sliced carrot
¹/₂ cup sliced celery
¹/₄ cup chopped onion
1¹/₂ teaspoons salt
¹/₄ teaspoon pepper
¹/₄ cup butter
¹/₄ cup flour
2 cups milk
2 cups shredded sharp
    Cheddar cheese
8 slices bacon, crisp-fried, crumbled

🐟 Combine the potatoes, water, carrot, celery, onion, salt and pepper in a 2-quart saucepan. Simmer, covered, for 10 minutes.

🐟 Melt the butter in a medium saucepan. Stir in the flour. Cook until bubbly, stirring constantly; do not brown.

🐟 Stir the milk into the flour mixture. Cook until thickened, stirring constantly. Add the cheese. Cook until the cheese melts, stirring to blend well.

🐟 Add to the potato mixture. Cook until heated through, stirring to blend well.

🐟 Ladle into soup bowls. Sprinkle with the bacon.

🐟

*This soup is popular for tailgate parties, brunches and winter luncheons, or serve it in mugs as a first course after snowy winter parties.*

🐟

# POTATO AND ASPARAGUS SOUP WITH CHEESE

*Yield: 4 to 6 servings*

*3 medium potatoes, peeled or*
*  unpeeled, cubed (3 cups)*
*1 (14-ounce) can chicken broth or*
*  1³/₄ cups fresh chicken broth*
*¹/₃ cup chopped onion*
*¹/₈ teaspoon nutmeg*
*1 teaspoon salt*
*1 (10-ounce) package frozen*
*  cut asparagus*
*1¹/₂ cups half-and-half*
*1 (5-ounce) jar Neufchâtel cheese*
*  with pimento, or 4 ounces*
*  whipped cream cheese*
*  with pimento*

## Garnish
*Croutons*

☞ Combine the potatoes, chicken broth, onion, nutmeg and salt in a 2-quart saucepan. Bring to a boil and reduce the heat. Simmer, covered, for 8 to 10 minutes or until the potatoes are tender.

☞ Add the asparagus. Bring to a boil and reduce the heat. Simmer for 5 to 8 minutes or until the vegetables are tender.

☞ Blend the half-and-half with the cheese spread in a bowl. Add to the soup. Cook until heated through, stirring until smooth; do not boil.

☞ Ladle into soup bowls. Garnish with croutons.

## Idaho-Iowa Corn and Potato Chowder

*Yield: 6 to 8 servings*

*3 slices bacon, diced*
*1 pound chicken*
*³/₄ cup chopped onion*
*³/₄ cup chopped celery*
*4 cups whole kernel corn*
*4 cups chicken broth*
*2 cups cubed potatoes*
*Salt to taste*
*1 cup whipping cream*
*2 tablespoons chopped parsley*
*Pepper to taste*

☞ Brown the bacon in a heavy saucepan. Remove the bacon to a paper towel and drain the saucepan, reserving 2 tablespoons drippings.

☞ Cut the chicken into cubes. Add the chicken, onion and celery to the drippings in the saucepan. Cook for 10 to 15 minutes or until the chicken and vegetables are tender, stirring constantly.

☞ Combine 2 cups of the corn and 1 cup of the chicken broth in a blender container; process until smooth.

☞ Add the puréed corn, the remaining broth, the remaining corn, potatoes and salt to the chicken mixture. Bring to a boil and reduce the heat. Simmer for 30 minutes or until the potatoes are tender.

☞ Stir in the cream and parsley. Simmer for 5 minutes. Add the bacon, salt and pepper. Ladle into soup bowls.

### BEAUTY TIPS
To darken your hair, comb warm or cooled potato water from boiled potatoes through your hair.

# Cheese and Vegetable Soup en Croûte

*Yield: 6 servings*

1 large bunch broccoli
1 cup chopped onion
$^{1}/_{2}$ cup melted butter
1 cup (1-inch) potato cubes
$^{1}/_{2}$ cup flour
4 (14 ounces each) cans
    chicken broth
$^{1}/_{2}$ cup whipping cream
$^{1}/_{4}$ teaspoon nutmeg
$^{1}/_{4}$ teaspoon salt
$^{1}/_{4}$ teaspoon pepper
1 cup shredded smoked or plain
    Cheddar cheese
6 frozen puff pastry shells, thawed
1 egg, beaten

Remove and reserve the broccoli florets. Chop the stems.

Sauté the onion in the butter in a large saucepan over medium heat for 5 minutes. Add the chopped broccoli stems and potatoes. Cook for 5 minutes.

Stir in the flour. Cook for 5 minutes, stirring constantly. Stir in the chicken broth. Bring to a boil, stirring constantly; reduce the heat. Simmer for 15 minutes.

Process in small batches in the blender. Strain into a clean saucepan.

Cook the broccoli florets in boiling salted water to cover in a saucepan for 2 minutes. Drain and add to the soup.

Bring the cream just to a boil in a small saucepan. Stir in the nutmeg, salt, pepper and $^{1}/_{4}$ cup of the cheese. Cook just until the cheese melts; do not boil. Stir into the soup. Spoon into 6 ovenproof soup bowls. Sprinkle with the remaining cheese.

Roll the puff pastry shells into circles 2 inches larger than the tops of the soup bowls. Brush the rims of the soup bowls with beaten egg. Place the pastry circles on the tops of the bowls and press to seal.

Place the bowls on a baking sheet. Bake at 400 degrees for 12 to 14 minutes or until golden brown.

*Note: This is worth the time it takes to prepare!*

 POTATO LEEK SOUP

*Yield: 4 to 6 servings*

*3 medium russet potatoes, peeled,*
*    cut into 1-inch pieces*
*3 cups chopped leeks*
*1 rib celery, chopped*
*1 large carrot, chopped*
*¼ cup butter*
*¾ teaspoon salt*
*½ cup stock or water*
*3 cups milk*
*Chopped fresh herbs such as thyme,*
*    marjoram or basil (optional)*
*Freshly ground pepper to taste*

🍠 Combine the potatoes with the leeks, celery, carrot, butter and salt in a large saucepan. Cook over medium heat for 5 minutes or until the butter melts and the vegetables are well coated.

🍠 Add the stock. Bring to a boil and reduce the heat. Simmer, covered, for 20 to 30 minutes or until the potatoes are tender, adding additional stock if needed.

🍠 Process the vegetable mixture with the milk in a blender until very smooth. Return to the saucepan. Add the fresh herbs and pepper.

🍠 Cook, covered, just until heated through; do not boil. Ladle into soup bowls and serve immediately.

POTATO TRIVIA

It would take

393,779,549 four-inch

French fries to go

around the earth's

equator end to end.

## Roasted Garlic and Two-Potato Soup

*Yield: 4 servings*

4 medium red potatoes
1 large onion, coarsely chopped
2 teaspoons chopped fresh rosemary,
    or 1 teaspoon crushed
    dried rosemary
1 whole bulb garlic
1 tablespoon olive oil
1 (14½-ounce) can chicken broth
1 tablespoon flour
½ teaspoon pepper
1 cup half-and-half

## Garnish
*Croutons*

☞ Peel and cube 2 of the potatoes; place on 1 side of a 9x9-inch baking pan. Cube the remaining 2 potatoes with skins; place on the other side of the baking pan. Sprinkle with the onion and rosemary.

☞ Slice off the pointed end of the bulb of garlic to expose the cloves; discard the papery skin. Place cut side up on top of the potatoes. Drizzle the entire mixture with olive oil.

☞ Bake, covered, at 400 degrees for 50 minutes or until the garlic and potatoes are tender.

☞ Squeeze the garlic cloves out of their skins. Combine with the peeled potatoes, half the onion, ¾ cup of the chicken broth, flour and pepper in a blender container. Process until coarsely puréed.

☞ Combine with the unpeeled potato, remaining onion, remaining broth and half-and-half in a 2-quart saucepan. Cook over medium heat until slightly thickened, stirring constantly.

☞ Ladle into soup bowls and garnish with croutons.

# Baked Potato Soup

From Chef Tim Holley of
Boise, Idaho

*Yield: 10 to 12 servings*

10 russet potatoes
3 leeks, chopped
2 medium yellow onions, diced
4 to 6 cloves of garlic,
    finely chopped
1/4 cup butter
1 teaspoon nutmeg
2 tablespoons (or more) salt
2 teaspoons pepper
8 cups canned or fresh chicken stock
1/2 cup whipping cream

## Garnish
*Bacon, chopped, crisp-fried*
*Sliced green onions*
*Grated Cheddar cheese*

➤ Bake the potatoes at 425 degrees for 45 to 60 minutes or until tender. Cool to room temperature. Scoop out and reserve the pulp.

➤ Sauté the leeks, onions and garlic in the butter in a saucepan for 10 minutes or until translucent.

➤ Add the potato pulp, nutmeg, salt and pepper. Stir in the chicken stock. Bring to a boil and reduce the heat to medium. Cook for 20 minutes, mashing the potato pulp against the side of the saucepan.

➤ Remove from the heat and stir in the cream. Adjust the seasonings. Ladle into soup bowls. Garnish with the bacon, green onions and cheese.

## COOKING TIP

To thicken soups, grate 3 tablespoons of raw potato for each cup of soup and simmer until the potato is absorbed, about 15 minutes.

## MINUTE MINESTRONE

*Yield: 4 servings*

3/4 *cup chopped onion*
*2 to 3 cloves of garlic, minced*
*1 tablespoon vegetable oil*
*2 (14 1/2 ounces each) cans vegetable broth*
2/3 *pound potatoes, cut into* 1/2-*inch cubes (2 medium potatoes)*
1 1/2 *cups frozen Italian mixed vegetables or mixed vegetables of choice*
*1 (8*3/4-*ounce) can red kidney beans, drained*
*1 (15-ounce) can chopped tomatoes*
*1 teaspoon dried Italian herb seasoning*
*Grated Parmesan cheese*

🖝 Sauté the onion and garlic in the oil in a 3-quart saucepan over medium heat until tender.

🖝 Add the vegetable broth and potatoes. Bring to a boil and reduce the heat. Simmer, covered, for 10 minutes or until the potatoes are tender.

🖝 Add the mixed vegetables, kidney beans, tomatoes and Italian seasoning. Simmer, covered, for 10 minutes.

🖝 Ladle into soup bowls. Sprinkle with the cheese. Serve with soft bread sticks and leafy green salad.

## Ham and Split Pea Soup

*Yield: 4 to 6 servings*

*8 ounces dried green or yellow*
   *split peas*
*1/2 cup chopped onion*
*1 rib celery, thinly sliced*
*1 medium carrot, shredded*
*1 cup cubed ham*
*1 beef bouillon cube*
*1/2 large or 1 small bay leaf*
*Salt and freshly ground pepper*
   *to taste*
*7 cups (about) water*
*1 medium potato, diced*
   *(about 1 cup)*

### Garnish
*Sour cream*
*Carrot curls*

✒ Rinse and sort the peas. Combine with the onion, celery, shredded carrot, ham, bouillon cube, bay leaf, salt and pepper in a 2-quart saucepan. Add the water.

✒ Bring to a boil and reduce the heat. Simmer for 1½ hours, stirring occasionally and adding additional water if needed.

✒ Add the potato. Cook for 30 minutes or longer or until the mixture is thickened to the desired consistency. Discard the bay leaf.

✒ Ladle into soup bowls. Garnish with dollops of sour cream and carrot curls. Serve with fresh fruit and crusty bread.

### POTATO TRIVIA

Potatoes are used in
making cosmetics,
paper, blood plasma,
fuel, biodegradable
packaging, animal
feed, and ice cream.

# Salads

## BOISE, THE CITY OF TREES

Nestled in the shadow of the Rocky Mountains with a pristine river flowing through its center, Boise traces its roots back to pioneer fur traders.

Where did Boise get its name? A popular legend that sounds logical is that French fur traders came to the edge of the desert plateau and looked down into the valley, its river and trees. They shouted, "Les Bois," and Boise has since been known as the City of Trees.

Then, British fur traders established a trading post known as Fort Boise in 1834 at the mouth of the Boise River, 40 miles from the present-day city. Twenty years later, due to frequent Indian raids, the original Fort Boise was abandoned. Despite this, the government wanted to build an official military fort in the area.

Before the plan could go into effect, gold was discovered in the Boise Basin in 1862. The military chose a new location for Fort Boise in 1863, and construction began. The townsite next to the fort would be protected, so the town grew quickly.

Adding to the gold-rush travelers were thousands of settlers who followed the Oregon Trail heading west.

In Idaho the trail went from the Idaho-Wyoming border to Bear Valley to Fort Hall and then followed the Snake River until it reached the Boise River. To this day, wheel ruts still can be seen along various spots of its path.

Meanwhile, routes to the Boise Basin and Owyhee mines crossed the Oregon Trail at the Fort Boise location. Because it was located at these major crossroads, Boise became a prosperous commercial center.

When the territorial legislature held its second session in 1864 in Lewiston, Boise was incorporated as a city and proclaimed the capital of Idaho Territory. This same year, on July 26, the *Idaho Statesman* newspaper produced its first edition and became the second newspaper in Idaho.

After the gold rush, Boise's population declined from 1,658 citizens in 1864 to 995 in 1870. But with new construction, including the territorial prison in 1869 and the United States Assay Office in 1872, Boise began to grow again. The capitol building in 1886 and a street car system the next year spurred Boise's growth. A few years later, in 1890, Idaho became a state.

Also increasing the population was a large migration of Basques from their native homes in the northern provinces of Spain. These proud people became the state's primary sheepherders, caring for the flocks of what was a major industry at that time. Basques gradually moved into the mainstream of city life in Boise, bringing their colorful culture with them. Today, the only Basque Museum in the United States is located in Boise. The area has the largest concentration of Basques outside of Spain.

Boise still remains the largest metropolitan community in the state. Numerous large businesses have their headquarters in the city. Some of these are Hewlett Packard, Boise Cascade, J.R. Simplot Company, Ore-Ida, Albertson's, Micron, and Morrison-Knudson. Boise is the hub of commerce, banking and government for the state.

Boise's lower elevation and moderate climate add to the quality of life. It is 2,842 feet above sea level. Snow storms may blanket nearby mountains during the winter but usually bring only rain to the valley. Summer temperatures can go into the 90s, but the low humidity and cool evenings make glorious weather. The annual average temperature is 62.8 degrees Fahrenheit.

Boise is home to the state's largest university, Boise State University. It is only 16 miles up a paved road to Bogus Basin Ski Area. Water-skiing at Lucky Peak Reservoir is just a few miles away. Floating in inner tubes on the Boise River is a popular summer activity. There are tennis courts and golf courses, plus opportunities for other outdoor sports.

There are many art organizations and museums, with modern facilities for exhibits, Broadway shows, ballet and other activities befitting a capital city.

## GREATEST POTATO SALAD

From Marie D. Galyean, Food Editor for the *Idaho Press-Tribune*, Nampa, Idaho

*Yield: 6 to 8 servings*

4 to 6 Idaho potatoes, peeled, cut
    into quarters
3 hard-cooked eggs, peeled, divided
1 medium onion, finely chopped
2 to 3 ribs celery, chopped
3 slices bacon, crisp-fried, crumbled
4 sweet pickle slices, chopped
1¹/₂ teaspoons lime juice or
    lemon juice
1 teaspoon mustard
¹/₄ teaspoon garlic powder
4 drops of Tabasco sauce or other
    red pepper sauce
1 to 1¹/₂ cups mayonnaise
¹/₂ teaspoon paprika

### Garnish
*Pimento strips*

☛ The day before serving, or early in the morning, boil the potatoes in water to cover in a saucepan for 20 minutes or just until fork-tender. Drain and let cool to room temperature or cooler. Cut into your choice of large or small dice.

☛ Chop 2 of the eggs. Combine with half the potatoes in a large serving bowl. Stir in half the onion, celery, bacon, pickles, lime juice, mustard, garlic powder, Tabasco sauce and mayonnaise and mix well. Add the remaining potatoes, onion, celery, bacon, pickles, lime juice, mustard, garlic powder, Tabasco sauce and mayonnaise and mix well. Smooth the top of the salad.

☛ Slice the remaining egg. Arrange the slices around the edge of the bowl. Sprinkle lightly with the paprika. Chill, covered, until serving time.

☛ Garnish with pimento strips.

## SOUTHWESTERN POTATO SALAD

*Yield: 8 servings*

5 medium russet potatoes
¹/₂ cup vegetable oil or olive oil
¹/₄ cup red wine vinegar
1 (1-ounce) envelope taco
   seasoning mix
1 (7-ounce) can whole kernel corn,
   drained
²/₃ cup diced celery
²/₃ cup shredded carrot
²/₃ cup diced green bell pepper
2 (2 ounces each) cans sliced black
   olives, drained
¹/₂ cup chopped red onion
2 tomatoes, cut into bite-size pieces
¹/₄ cup chopped cilantro

🥄 Cook the potatoes in boiling water
in a saucepan for 30 minutes or until
tender; drain. Cool slightly and cut
into cubes.

🥄 Mix the oil, vinegar and taco
seasoning mix in a small bowl.
Combine with the potatoes in a large
bowl and toss gently to coat. Marinate,
covered, in the refrigerator for 1 hour.

🥄 Fold in the corn, celery, carrot,
green pepper, olives, onion, tomatoes
and cilantro. Chill until serving time.

🥄

*This makes a great salad for
outdoor picnics.*

🥄

 ## Homespun German Potato Salad

*Yield: 8 servings*

6 medium russet potatoes, peeled,
    cut into quarters
$1/4$ medium onion, chopped
Salt to taste
Dressing

### Dressing
5 slices bacon
1 tablespoon flour
$3/4$ cup water
$1/2$ cup vinegar
$1/2$ cup sugar
1 teaspoon salt
$1/2$ teaspoon pepper
2 eggs, beaten

Combine the potatoes and onion in a saucepan. Sprinkle with salt. Add enough water to cover. Boil over medium-high heat just until tender. Drain and let cool. If desired, reserve the cooking liquid to add additional flavor to the dressing. The potatoes may be prepared 2 to 3 days ahead and stored in the refrigerator until needed.

For the dressing, fry the bacon in an 8- to 10-inch skillet until crisp. Add the flour gradually, stirring until dissolved. Stir in the water, vinegar and sugar. Add the salt and pepper. Stir a small amount of the hot mixture into the eggs; stir the eggs into the hot mixture. Cook until thickened, stirring constantly. Remove from the heat and cool slightly.

Cut the potato quarters into $1/4$- to $1/2$-inch slices. Layer the potato slices and dressing $1/3$ at a time in a 3-quart casserole. At this point, the salad may be stored in the refrigerator for up to 1 day.

Heat for 30 minutes or until heated through in a 350-degree oven. Serve warm.

*The sweet-and-sour flavors of this warm salad are great when the salad is served with bratwurst, hot dogs or other grilled sausages.*

# Peanut Potato Salad

*Yield: 6 to 8 servings*

3 pounds red potatoes
12 slices bacon, crisp-fried,
    crumbled
1 cup salted Spanish peanuts
1 medium red bell pepper, chopped
2 ribs celery, chopped
4 green onions, chopped
$^1/_4$ cup chopped cilantro
$^1/_4$ cup chopped parsley
*Dressing*
Salt and pepper to taste

## Dressing
$^3/_4$ cup mayonnaise
$^1/_2$ cup chunky peanut butter
3 tablespoons cider vinegar

🖎 Boil the potatoes in water to cover in a saucepan until tender. Drain and let cool. Cut into 1-inch cubes.

🖎 Combine the potatoes, bacon, peanuts, red pepper, celery, green onions, cilantro and parsley in a large bowl and mix well.

🖎 For the dressing, whisk the mayonnaise, peanut butter and vinegar in a small bowl. Pour over the salad. Season with salt and pepper.

# CORNED BEEF POTATO SALAD

*Yield: 6 to 8 servings*

2 pounds red potatoes, cut into
   *¹/₂-inch pieces*
*¹/₄ cup sweet pickle relish*
*2 tablespoons white vinegar*
*1¹/₂ teaspoons celery seeds*
*Salt and pepper to taste*
*1¹/₂ cups diced cooked corned beef*
*1 cup chopped green onions*
*1 cup chopped celery*
*4 to 6 tablespoons mayonnaise*

## Garnish
*3 hard-cooked eggs,*
   *cut into quarters*

☞ Cook the potatoes in boiling salted water to cover in a saucepan for 10 minutes or just until tender; drain. Let cool for 10 minutes.

☞ Combine the potatoes, relish, vinegar and celery seeds in a large bowl and toss to blend. Season generously with salt and pepper.

☞ Add the corned beef, green onions and celery and mix well. Add enough mayonnaise to hold the salad together and mix well.

☞ Garnish with the eggs.

☞ Serve immediately or cover and store in the refrigerator for up to 1 day.

## COOKING TIP

Potato salads are best when the dressing is added to warm potatoes. Otherwise, the potatoes will not absorb as much dressing, resulting in a less flavorful salad.

## COOKING TIP

To have nice firm potato chunks for salads, be careful when you cut them vertically and horizontally. The closer to a 90-degree angle they are cut, the firmer they will stay when boiling. If the potato chunks are cut "any old way," those weird points mush up faster when cooking.

# CURRIED POTATO SALAD

*Yield: 6 to 8 servings*

2 pounds red potatoes
²/₃ cup raisins
14 slices bacon, crisp-fried, crumbled
6 tablespoons finely chopped red onion
1 cup chopped green apple
2 bananas, cut into ¹/₄-inch slices
²/₃ cup unsalted peanuts
¹/₂ cup shredded unsweetened coconut
*Dressing*
1 cup chopped fresh mint

## Dressing
1 to 1¹/₂ cups mayonnaise or low-fat mayonnaise
2 tablespoons mild curry powder

## Garnish
*Sprigs of fresh mint*

🐟 Boil the potatoes in water to cover in a saucepan until tender; drain. Cut into cubes.

🐟 Combine the potatoes, raisins, bacon, onion, apple, bananas, peanuts and coconut in a large bowl and toss lightly.

🐟 Mix the mayonnaise and curry powder in a small bowl. Stir the dressing and the chopped mint gently into the potato mixture.

🐟 Chill, covered, until serving time.

🐟 Garnish with fresh mint sprigs.

# Easy Hot Potato Salad

*Yield: 4 servings*

1 (5-ounce) package instant
    *scalloped potatoes*
*3 cups water*
*1 teaspoon salt*
*1 tablespoon instant minced onion*
*6 slices bacon*
*1 cup milk*
*$^1/_3$ cup mayonnaise or mayonnaise-*
    *type salad dressing*
*2 tablespoons vinegar*
*1 teaspoon prepared yellow mustard*

☞ Combine the potatoes, water, salt
and onion in a saucepan. Cook for
5 minutes or until almost tender;
drain well.

☞ Fry the bacon in a skillet until
crisp. Drain the skillet, reserving
1 tablespoon of the bacon drippings.
Crumble the bacon.

☞ Combine the sauce mix from the
instant potatoes, milk, mayonnaise,
vinegar and mustard in a bowl and
mix until smooth.

☞ Combine the milk mixture, potato
mixture, bacon and reserved drippings
in a large bowl, stirring just until
mixed. Spoon into a baking dish.

☞ Bake, covered, at 350 degrees for
45 minutes.

## Cooking Tip

If you have added too
much mayonnaise
dressing to potato
salad, yet the taste is
good, mix in a few
potato flakes. The
flakes will absorb
moisture from the
dressing without
changing the taste.
They thicken up
the salad.

## Papaya Potato Salad with Chutney Vinaigrette

*Yield: 8 servings*

2 pounds red potatoes, cubed
1 (8-ounce) ripe papaya
8 ounces cherry tomatoes,
    cut into halves
*¹/₂ cup celery slices, cut into
    ¹/₄-inch pieces*
*¹/₂ cup finely chopped red onion*
*Chutney Vinaigrette*
*Lettuce leaves*
*¹/₄ cup shredded sweetened coconut,
    toasted (see Note)*

### Chutney Vinaigrette
*¹/₄ cup vegetable oil*
*2 tablespoons lime juice*
*2 tablespoons white wine vinegar*
*2 tablespoons prepared
    mango chutney*
*1 jalapeño, seeded, minced*
*1 tablespoon chopped cilantro*
*Salt to taste*

🌿 Cook the potatoes in water to cover in a saucepan until tender. Drain and let cool. Do not peel.

🌿 Slice the papaya into halves. Seed, peel and cut each half into cubes.

🌿 Combine the potatoes, tomatoes, celery, papaya and onion in a large bowl and mix well.

🌿 For the vinaigrette, mix the oil, lime juice, vinegar, chutney, jalapeño, cilantro and salt in a small bowl.

🌿 Add the vinaigrette to the salad and mix well. Chill thoroughly.

🌿 To serve, place ³/₄ cup salad on each lettuce-lined plate. Sprinkle with the coconut.

🌿 This is a great summer recipe to accompany watermelon, corn on the cob and whatever else is on the grill.

🌿

*Note: To toast coconut, spread in a single layer on a baking sheet. Bake at 375 degrees for 10 minutes or until lightly browned, tossing occasionally.*

🌿

## Sweet Onion Potato Salad

From Karen Mangum, MS, RD,
author of *Life's Simple Pleasures,
Fine Vegetarian Cooking for
Sharing and Celebration*

*Yield: 10 servings*

3 medium red potatoes
1 large sweet white onion, cut into
    quarters, thinly sliced
³/₄ cup thinly sliced celery
1 large Golden Delicious apple,
    cored, diced
¹/₄ cup chopped black olives
¹/₃ cup chopped sweet pickles
1 cup plain low-fat yogurt
¹/₂ cup reduced-calorie mayonnaise
2 tablespoons Dijon mustard
2 tablespoons fresh lemon juice
1 teaspoon reduced-sodium
    soy sauce
Salt and pepper to taste

🖝 Boil the potatoes in water to cover
in a saucepan for 30 minutes or until
tender. Drain and cool. Cut into cubes.
🖝 Combine the potatoes, onion,
celery, apple, olives and pickles in a
large bowl and mix well.
🖝 Mix the yogurt, mayonnaise, Dijon
mustard, lemon juice and soy sauce in
a small bowl. Season with salt and
pepper and mix gently.
🖝 Fold the yogurt mixture into the
potato mixture.
🖝 Chill, covered, for 4 hours
or longer.

### Shoe Renewer

Rub a raw potato over

badly scuffed shoes,

polish them, and then

admire the new shine

to your shoes.

## Hawaiian Sweet Potato Salad

*Yield: 4 to 6 servings*

8 ounces bacon, cut into
    $^1/_2$-inch pieces
3 cups cooked sweet potatoes
2 cups pineapple chunks
$^1/_2$ cup mayonnaise
1 tablespoon Dijon mustard
2 tablespoons fresh lime juice
$^1/_2$ teaspoon pepper
$^1/_2$ cup chopped macadamia nuts
Romaine lettuce (optional)

### Garnish
*Pineapple ring*
*Lime twist*

☛ Fry the bacon in a skillet until crisp; drain. Crumble the bacon. Mix with the sweet potatoes and pineapple in a large bowl.

☛ Mix the mayonnaise, Dijon mustard, lime juice and pepper in a small bowl. Add to the sweet potato mixture and toss gently.

☛ Stir in the macadamia nuts.

☛ Serve in a lettuce-lined bowl. Garnish with a pineapple ring and twist of lime.

☛ This recipe is also a hit with non-sweet-potato lovers.


## Caesar Potato Salad

From the Simplot Kitchens in Caldwell, Idaho

*Yield: 10 servings*

6 cups ($1^1/_2$ pounds) frozen Simplot
    Recipe Quick Potatoes (see Note)
3 hard-cooked eggs, chopped
2 tablespoons black olives,
    drained, sliced
$^1/_3$ cup crumbled crisp-fried bacon
$^1/_3$ cup thinly sliced green onions
2 cups creamy Italian salad dressing
$^3/_4$ cup freshly grated
    Parmesan cheese
1 cup blanched broccoli florets

☛ Place the potatoes in boiling water to cover in a saucepan. Cover and return to a boil; reduce the heat. Simmer for 40 to 50 minutes or until very tender; drain. (The potatoes need to be cooked this long because the vinegar in the dressing will increase the firmness of the cooked potatoes.)

☛ Combine the potatoes, eggs, olives, bacon and green onions in a large bowl and mix well. Stir in a mixture of the salad dressing and cheese. Chill thoroughly.

☛ Stir in the broccoli just before serving.

☛

*Note: You may substitute $1^1/_2$ pounds fresh potatoes cut into $^1/_2$-inch pieces for the frozen potatoes.*

☛

## POTATO AND FRESH ASPARAGUS SALAD IN BASIL MINT DRESSING

*Yield: 4 to 6 servings*

1 pound russet potatoes
1 pound fresh asparagus, broken
    into 2-inch pieces
*Basil Mint Dressing*
*Butter lettuce leaves*

### Basil Mint Dressing
*$^1/_4$ cup olive oil*
*$^1/_4$ cup corn oil or vegetable oil*
*$^1/_4$ cup fresh lemon juice*
*1 clove of garlic, pressed*
*2 tablespoons chopped fresh mint*
*2 tablespoons chopped fresh basil*
*$^3/_4$ teaspoon salt*
*$^1/_4$ teaspoon pepper*

🖙 Combine the potatoes with cold water to cover in a saucepan. Bring to a boil; reduce the heat. Simmer until the potatoes are tender. Peel the potatoes while warm; cut into $^1/_2$-inch slices.

🖙 Cook the asparagus in boiling salted water in a saucepan for 5 to 7 minutes or until tender-crisp; drain.

🖙 Toss the asparagus with the potatoes in a large bowl.

🖙 For the dressing, whisk the olive oil, corn oil, lemon juice, garlic, mint, basil, salt and pepper in a medium bowl. Pour over the warm vegetables. Let stand at room temperature for 1 hour.

🖙 Line a shallow serving dish with lettuce leaves. Arrange the potato slices and asparagus pieces in overlapping rows over the lettuce.

🖙 Serve with grilled chicken or fish.

# CHICKEN, NEW POTATO AND PASTA SALAD

*Yield: 6 to 8 servings*

*10 small red potatoes (1¹/₄ pounds)*
*2 tablespoons olive oil or vegetable oil, divided*
*¹/₂ teaspoon salt, divided*
*1¹/₂ cups penne or corkscrew macaroni*
*4 large chicken breast halves, cut into 1-inch strips*
*¹/₄ teaspoon pepper*
*Dressing*
*1 cup chopped broccoli*
*¹/₂ cup chopped carrot*
*¹/₂ cup sliced black olives*
*2 tablespoons grated Parmesan cheese*

## Dressing

*1 teaspoon grated lemon zest*
*2 tablespoons fresh lemon juice*
*¹/₂ teaspoon sugar*
*2 tablespoons olive oil*
*1 teaspoon salt*
*¹/₄ teaspoon pepper*

🐟 Cut the potatoes into halves. Toss with 1 tablespoon of the olive oil and ¹/₄ teaspoon of the salt in a 9x9-inch baking pan. Roast at 450 degrees for 25 minutes.

🐟 Cook the pasta using the package directions; drain.

🐟 Rinse the chicken and pat dry. Heat the remaining 1 tablespoon of the olive oil in a 10-inch skillet. Add the chicken. Season with the remaining ¹/₄ teaspoon salt and pepper. Cook over medium heat until the chicken is cooked through.

🐟 For the dressing, whisk the lemon zest, lemon juice, sugar, olive oil, salt and pepper in a large bowl.

🐟 Add the potatoes, pasta, chicken, broccoli, carrot, olives and cheese and toss well.

🐟 Serve warm or cold with a crusty bread.

# GRILLED TUNA SALAD

*Yield: 4 servings*

## Dressing

$^1/_4$ cup extra-virgin olive oil
2 tablespoons balsamic vinegar
1 tablespoon water or wine
1 to 2 cloves of garlic, finely minced
$^1/_4$ teaspoon pepper
2 tablespoons minced
    fresh rosemary

## Salad

8 small new red potatoes
$^1/_2$ cup water, divided
1 pound fresh green beans
8 firm fresh plum tomatoes,
    cut into quarters
$^1/_4$ cup black Greek olives
4 (6 ounces each) tuna steaks,
    1 inch thick
1 teaspoon lemon pepper
8 cups mixed spring green lettuces
$^1/_2$ red onion, thinly sliced
2 tablespoons minced fresh parsley

🐟 For the dressing, combine the olive oil, vinegar, water, garlic, pepper and rosemary in a jar. Shake vigorously until well blended.

🐟 For the salad, scrub the potatoes and prick with a fork. Combine with $^1/_4$ cup of the water in a glass bowl. Microwave, covered with vented plastic wrap, on High for 10 minutes; drain. Cover and set aside.

🐟 Rinse the green beans. Break into bite-size pieces and cut off the stems. Combine with the remaining $^1/_4$ cup water in a glass bowl. Microwave, covered with vented plastic wrap, on High for 12 minutes; drain. Mix with the cooked potatoes. Cool to room temperature.

🐟 Add the tomatoes and olives to the potato mixture. Pour half the dressing over the tomato mixture. Marinate for 30 minutes.

🐟 Grease the grill with nonstick cooking spray. Sprinkle the tuna steaks generously with lemon pepper. Grill on hot grill for 3 to 5 minutes or until the edges of the steaks begin to turn white. Turn and grill for 3 minutes longer for medium or 5 minutes longer for well done.

🐟 Arrange the lettuce on 4 large plates. Place a large serving of the vegetables along each side of the plate. Arrange the onion over the lettuce.

🐟 Place the steaks over the onion. Sprinkle with the parsley. Add the remaining dressing or serve it on the side.

# RED POTATO AND RED SALMON SALAD

*Yield: 4 servings*

5 to 6 red potatoes (see Note)
1 (15-ounce) can red sockeye
    salmon, drained
2 to 3 cloves of garlic, minced
2 tablespoons chopped basil leaves
$^1/_4$ cup chopped red onion
$^1/_2$ cup chopped celery
2 teaspoons Dijon mustard
$^1/_4$ cup balsamic vinegar
Red lettuce leaves, rinsed, chilled

🍃 Steam the potatoes until tender. Cut into quarters.
🍃 Flake the salmon into a medium bowl. Add the garlic, basil, onion, celery and potatoes. Drizzle with a mixture of the mustard and vinegar and toss to coat.

🍃 Arrange the lettuce on serving plates. Spoon the salad onto the lettuce.

🍃

*Note: If in a hurry, substitute a 15-ounce can of whole new potatoes. Drain well and cut the potatoes into quarters.*

🍃

#  SALADE NIÇOISE

*Yield: 4 to 6 servings*

2 pounds new potatoes
Dressing
1 (14-ounce) can artichoke hearts
2 cups fresh green beans
Salad greens
2 (7 ounces each) cans albacore
    tuna, drained (see Note)
1 pint cherry tomatoes
1 cup pitted black olives (optional)
3 hard-cooked eggs, cut into
    quarters
¹/₂ cup canned or bottled
    pimento strips
1 large green bell pepper,
    cut into rings
1 (2-ounce) can anchovies
    (optional)
2 tablespoons capers, drained

## Dressing

1 cup olive oil
¹/₂ cup tarragon vinegar
¹/₄ cup fresh lemon juice
2 cloves of garlic, crushed
1 tablespoon dry mustard
1 teaspoon sugar
¹/₂ tablespoon salt
Freshly ground pepper to taste

## Garnish

¹/₄ cup chopped parsley

🖝 Boil the potatoes in water to cover in a saucepan just until tender. Drain and let cool. Cut into slices.

🖝 For the dressing, combine the olive oil, vinegar, lemon juice, garlic, mustard, sugar, salt and pepper in a blender container. Process until mixed.

🖝 Pour the dressing over the potatoes and artichoke hearts in a large bowl. Marinate for 2 hours or longer, stirring occasionally.

🖝 Cook the green beans in water to cover in a saucepan just until tender; drain. Chill until needed.

🖝 To serve, line a bowl with salad greens. Drain any excess dressing from the potato mixture and spoon the mixture onto the salad greens. Arrange the tuna in the center. Arrange the green beans, tomatoes, olives, eggs, pimento strips, green pepper, anchovies and capers around the top of the salad. Garnish with the parsley.

🖝

*Note: Omit the tuna if you want to serve this as a side dish. It is especially good with grilled lamb.*

🖝

# Entrées

## Basque Boarding Houses

In 1916, Jeri Echeverria's father left his family farm on the Spanish side of the Pyrenees Mountains and sailed across the Atlantic. When he got off the boat in America his daughter Jeri says he did what most Basque immigrants did: "They came out of Ellis Island and there would be somebody on the dock yelling

'Euskaldunak emen Badira?' Meaning, are there any Basques here?" Basque is such a unique language that only Basque people could understand the question. Echeverria says the new immigrants would be taken to the Basque boarding house on Cherry Street in New York City that was owned by Valentin Aquirre. Each new immigrant was told: "This is how you do it in America."

Aquirre would figure out the best train connections, pin a name tag on the immigrant's shirt along with his final destination, give him sandwiches and say, "Don't get off until you get to the switching station in Utah. Then look straight across the platform. Walk across to the Basque Hotel and they'll help you the rest of the way."

Many more Basques came to the United States in the 1930s because they were fleeing the Spanish Civil War. These descendants still live in the American West.

The first Basque immigrants usually were sheepherders. Barely a decade after they arrived, Basque women came and set up boarding houses in downtown Boise. Most have been torn down but one on Grove Street has been restored. There is original furniture inside this boarding house—a wood-burning stove, straight-backed chairs, trunks from the Old Country, the boarding house table and many framed photos of relatives. Jeri Echeverria, now a Basque historian at California State University, Fresno, who studies the role boarding houses played in the development of the American West says, "I know many old-timers who came to Boise and were told: Go to Basave's, or Go to Zapater's, or Mateo's (Big Mike's) and stay there till I find you."

After they were "found" by their relatives, sheepherders stayed on at Basque boarding houses because the owners, called *hoteleras,* became like parents to them and would store their supplies and mail. When a Basque sheepherder who had been working on the range was injured or sick, he would return to the boarding house and be cared for. In later years when that same Basque raised a family and got a ranch outside of town, his wife would come back to the boarding house and stay with the *hotelera* so the doctor would be near if there were childbirth complications.

Weddings, birthdays, anniversaries, baptism dinners, even wakes were held at the boarding houses. Many Basques joked, I was born in a boarding house, married there and died there.

Basque women played a strategic role in what most consider a male-dominated culture, says Echeverria. "Many Basques will tell you teasingly, that yes, the father rules the roost but it's the mother who has the power." In the Basque hotels the women took on a particularly strong role when their husbands were at the sheep camps.

Besides keeping the hotel books and caring for their own children, the Basque *hoteleras* also would cook and clean for up to thirty people a day, tend a garden, milk dairy cows, can vegetables and fruits, make sausage, brew wine and serve as translators when sheepherders had to go to the doctor.

Many *hoteleras* became matriarchs in their town, says Echeverria. "In Boise, the women of the Letemendi, Arregui, and Uberuaga families played particularly powerful roles in the community beyond the confines of their little hotels."

Echeverria says today the Basques are fully integrated into American culture but they continue to celebrate their heritage by performing dances dressed in traditional costumes, and teaching youngsters music, dance and the Basque language. Perhaps the strongest example of Basque pride in their culture is the historic boarding house, part of the Basques Museum complex next to the Basque Center in downtown Boise, which is maintained in excellent condition.

*— by Jyl Hoyt*

# Potato Roulade

*Yield: 6 servings*

*4 medium russet potatoes, cut into
    1-inch cubes*
*6 tablespoons butter or margarine,
    divided*
*1 tablespoon chopped fresh chives*
*Salt and pepper to taste*
*2 medium onions, chopped*
*1 pound lean ground beef*
*8 ounces ground pork*
*2 tablespoons freshly grated
    Parmesan cheese*
*2 tablespoons minced golden raisins*
*$^1/_2$ teaspoon dried oregano*
*$^1/_2$ cup bread crumbs*
*2 eggs, lightly beaten*
*1 tablespoon olive oil*

## Gravy (optional)
*Flour*
*Beef broth*

☞ Cook the potatoes in boiling water to cover in a saucepan over medium heat until tender; drain. Dry the potatoes over low heat in the saucepan. Peel and mash the potatoes. Combine the potatoes, 2 tablespoons of the butter, chives, salt and pepper in a bowl. Beat until smooth and fluffy.

☞ Melt 2 tablespoons of the butter in a saucepan. Add the onions. Cook for 5 minutes or until tender but not brown.

☞ Combine the onions, ground beef, ground pork, cheese, raisins, oregano, bread crumbs and eggs in a large bowl and mix well.

☞ Reserve $^1/_2$ cup of the meat mixture. Spread the remaining mixture $^1/_2$ inch thick on a large sheet of oiled waxed paper. Shape into a solid 7x10-inch rectangle. Spread the potato mixture smoothly and evenly over the meat mixture.

☞ Roll up the meat mixture with the waxed paper as for a jelly roll, completely encasing the potato mixture. Patch any holes with the reserved meat mixture; if there are no holes, pat onto the ends of the roll.

☞ Slide the roll carefully off the waxed paper into a lightly buttered shallow baking pan. Bake at 350 degrees for 1 hour. Heat the remaining 2 tablespoons butter and olive oil in a saucepan and use to baste the roll occasionally during baking.

☞ Remove the roll from the oven. Let stand for 5 minutes. Slice with a sharp serrated knife.

☞ Stir a small amount of flour and beef broth into the pan drippings to make gravy.

## QUICK AND DIFFERENT MEAT LOAF

Prepare and bake your favorite meat loaf. During the last few minutes baking time, pile mounds of fluffy whipped potatoes on top. Reduce the oven temperature to 300 degrees and cook until the potatoes are lightly browned. Sprinkle with Parmesan cheese before serving. By the way, did you know that you can substitute potato flakes for the bread crumbs in your meat loaf mixture?

## BEEF AND POTATO BURGERS

*Yield: 4 servings*

*8 ounces ground beef or
    ground turkey*
*3/4 cup grated frozen
    processed potatoes*
*1 (8-ounce) can julienne-style beets*
*2 eggs, lightly beaten, or 1/2 cup
    egg substitute*
*1/2 teaspoon salt*
*4 hamburger buns*

☞ Combine the ground beef, potatoes, beets, eggs and salt in a bowl and mix well. Shape into 4 patties.

☞ Broil 6 inches from the heat source for 20 minutes. Turn and broil for 10 minutes longer.

☞ Serve on buns with your choice of condiments.

☞ These patties may be cooked and then frozen. Reheat in the microwave.

# USTLER'S PIE

*Yield: 8 servings*

*7 russet potatoes, cut into*
*1-inch cubes*
*1 cup warm milk (2%, 1% or skim)*
*3¹/₂ teaspoons salt, divided*
*1 teaspoon pepper, divided*
*4 teaspoons butter, divided*
*4 cups shredded green cabbage*
*1¹/₂ cups chopped onion*
*2 teaspoons minced garlic*
*³/₄ teaspoon dried thyme leaves*
*2¹/₂ pounds lean ground beef*
*1 (2¹/₂-inch) bay leaf*
*1 (16-ounce) can crushed tomatoes*
*¹/₄ cup red wine (optional)*
*2 tablespoons flour*
*¹/₂ cup shredded Cheddar cheese*

🌱 Combine the potatoes with enough water to cover in a saucepan. Bring to a boil. Simmer for 15 minutes or until tender; drain. Return the potatoes to the saucepan. Heat over low heat for 2 minutes or until dry and floury, stirring constantly. Remove from the heat. Mash until almost smooth. Add the milk, 2 teaspoons of the salt and ¹/₂ teaspoon of the pepper. Beat until smooth and fluffy. Set aside.

🌱 Melt 2 teaspoons of the butter in a large saucepan over medium heat. Add the cabbage. Cook for 5 to 6 minutes or until tender, stirring constantly. Remove the cabbage and set aside.

🌱 Melt the remaining 2 teaspoons butter in the saucepan over medium-high heat. Add the onion, garlic and thyme. Sauté for 4 minutes.

🌱 Add the ground beef and bay leaf. Cook until the ground beef is browned and cooked through, stirring until crumbly.

🌱 Stir in the tomatoes, wine, flour, remaining 1¹/₂ teaspoons salt and ¹/₂ teaspoon pepper. Cook until slightly thickened. Remove and discard the bay leaf.

🌱 Pour the ground beef mixture into a 9x13-inch casserole and smooth the top. Fold the cabbage into the mashed potatoes. Spread over the top, completely covering the ground beef mixture. Sprinkle with the cheese.

🌱 Bake at 400 degrees for 35 minutes or until the ground beef mixture is heated through and the cheese and potatoes are golden brown.

 IDAHO STIR-FRY

*Yield: 4 servings*

12 to 16 ounces lean beef steak
8 ounces fresh green beans, cut into
    1¹/₂-inch slices
8 ounces small red potatoes,
    cut into quarters
2 tablespoons water
2 teaspoons olive oil
1 large onion, cut into halves, sliced
2 cloves of garlic, minced
8 ounces small mushrooms, sliced
¹/₄ cup oil-pack sun-dried tomatoes,
    drained, chopped
2 tablespoons chopped green onions
2 tablespoons balsamic vinegar
³/₄ teaspoon salt
¹/₄ teaspoon pepper

☞ Cut the steak crosswise into thin slices; set aside.

☞ Combine the green beans, potatoes and water in a 2-quart microwave-safe casserole. Microwave on High for 7 to 10 minutes or until the green beans are tender-crisp and the potatoes are tender, stirring once. Set aside without draining.

☞ Heat the olive oil in a 12-inch nonstick skillet over medium-high heat. Add the onion and garlic. Cook until the onion is translucent. Stir in the mushrooms and tomatoes. Cook until the mushrooms and tomatoes are lightly browned.

☞ Add the green bean mixture and its cooking liquid to the skillet. Cook over medium-high heat until the liquid is evaporated and the potatoes are lightly browned. Spoon onto a serving platter.

☞ Cook the steak slices in the skillet until browned, stirring quickly and constantly.

☞ Toss the steak slices, green onions, vinegar, salt and pepper with the cooked vegetable mixture.

## Two-Potato and Apricot Stew in a Pumpkin Shell

*Yield: 6 servings*

2 pounds lean beef stew meat, cut
    into 1¹/₂-inch cubes
1 large onion, chopped
2 cloves of garlic, minced
3 tablespoons vegetable oil
2 large tomatoes, chopped
1 large green bell pepper, chopped
1 tablespoon salt
¹/₂ teaspoon pepper
1 teaspoon sugar
1 cup dried apricots
3 white potatoes, peeled, diced
3 sweet potatoes, peeled, diced
2 cups beef broth
1 medium pumpkin
Melted butter
Salt and pepper to taste
¹/₄ cup dry sherry
1 (16-ounce) can whole kernel corn,
    drained

☙ Cook the beef, onion and garlic in the oil in a stockpot until the beef is browned. Add the tomatoes, green pepper, 1 tablespoon salt, ¹/₂ teaspoon pepper, sugar, apricots, potatoes, sweet potatoes and broth and mix well. Simmer, covered, for 1 hour.

☙ Cut off and discard the pumpkin top. Scoop out the seeds and stringy membrane. Brush the inside of the pumpkin with butter. Sprinkle lightly with salt and pepper to taste.

☙ Stir the sherry and corn into the stew. Spoon into the pumpkin shell. Place the pumpkin shell in a shallow baking pan. Bake at 325 degrees for 1 hour or until the pumpkin pulp is tender.

☙ Place the pumpkin in a large bowl to stabilize it on the table. Ladle the stew into individual bowls, scooping out some of the pumpkin with each serving of stew.

## POTATO TRIVIA

In times of hardship, workers have frequently accepted potatoes in place of money.

# ℰLK STEAK CASSEROLE

*Yield: 4 to 6 servings*

*¹/₂ cup (or more) flour*
*Salt and pepper to taste*
*2¹/₂ pounds elk steak, cut into 2- to*
  *3-inch pieces*
*1 tablespoon olive oil*
*1 medium onion, chopped*
*4 to 5 cloves of garlic, minced*
*3 medium russet potatoes, diced*
*4 carrots, cut into 1-inch slices*
*8 ounces sliced mushrooms*
*1 envelope onion soup mix*
*3 cups water*
*2 tablespoons Worcestershire sauce*
*¹/₂ to ³/₄ cup red wine*

☞ Mix the flour, salt and pepper in a shallow dish. Dredge the steak in the mixture.

☞ Heat the olive oil in a skillet. Add the steak, onion and garlic. Cook until the steak is browned. Pour into a large casserole. Add the potatoes, carrots and mushrooms.

☞ Mix the soup mix with the water, Worcestershire sauce and wine in a bowl. Pour over the vegetables.

☞ Bake, covered with foil, at 350 degrees for 2 hours or until the vegetables are tender.

#  CRUSTED LAMB AND POTATOES

*Yield: 6 servings*

1 leg of lamb, upper thigh half
   *(3 to 3¹/₂ pounds)*
*3 pounds russet potatoes, peeled,*
   *cut into ³/₄-inch slices*
*1¹/₂ cups chicken broth*

## Seasoning Paste

*3 cloves of garlic, minced*
*1 small onion, minced*
*3 tablespoons minced parsley*
*1 cup seasoned stuffing mix*
*3 tablespoons butter or margarine,*
   *at room temperature*
*1 tablespoon grated lemon zest*
*2 tablespoons lemon juice*
*Salt and pepper to taste*

☞ Trim any surface fat from the lamb.

☞ Cover the bottom of a 12x15-inch roasting pan with the potato slices. Pour in the broth. Set the lamb over the potatoes. Roast at 400 degrees for 45 minutes.

☞ For the seasoning paste, combine the garlic, onion, parsley, stuffing mix, butter, lemon zest and lemon juice in a bowl and mash well.

☞ Spread the paste evenly over the lamb and potatoes.

☞ Roast for 25 minutes longer or until the crust on the lamb is browned and a meat thermometer inserted in the thickest part of the lamb registers 145 degrees for medium-rare.

☞ Remove the lamb, potatoes and cooking liquid to a serving platter.

☞ Season with salt and pepper.

## SCARBOROUGH TENDERLOIN WITH OVEN-ROASTED POTATOES

. . . "Are you going to
Scarborough Fair?
Parsley, sage, rosemary,
and thyme . . ."

*Yield: 8 servings*

*¹/₃ cup olive oil*
*2 cloves of garlic, minced*
*2 teaspoons crushed dried*
*    rosemary leaves*
*2 teaspoons crushed dried*
*    thyme leaves*
*¹/₈ teaspoon sage*
*¹/₂ teaspoon salt*
*¹/₄ teaspoon pepper*
*2 (³/₄ to 1 pound each) whole pork*
*    tenderloins (see Note)*
*2¹/₂ pounds new potatoes,*
*    cut into quarters*

🖝 Mix the olive oil, garlic, rosemary, thyme, sage, salt and pepper in a bowl. Coat the pork with 3 tablespoons of the mixture and place in a large roasting pan. Toss the potatoes with the remaining herb mixture. Arrange the potatoes around the pork.

🖝 Roast at 375 degrees for 20 minutes. Stir the potatoes. Roast for 15 to 20 minutes longer or until a meat thermometer registers 155 degrees and the cooking juices run clear.

🖝 Broil on the top oven rack for 5 minutes or until browned.

🖝 Let stand for 5 minutes before slicing.

🖝

*Note: May substitute beef tenderloin for the pork.*

🖝

## PORK CHOPS O'BRIEN
From Ore-Ida Foods, Inc.

*Yield: 6 servings*

1 cup frozen Ore-Ida Onion Ringers,
    thawed
1 tablespoon vegetable oil
6 pork chops
*Seasoned salt to taste*
1 (10-ounce) can
    cream of celery soup
$^1/_2$ cup milk
$^1/_2$ cup sour cream
$^1/_4$ teaspoon pepper
$^1/_2$ teaspoon seasoned salt
1 (24-ounce) package Ore-Ida
    Potatoes O'Brien, thawed
1 cup shredded Cheddar cheese,
    divided
$^1/_2$ cup Ore-Ida frozen chopped
    onions, thawed

🐾 Fry or bake the Onion Ringers using the package directions. Let cool. Chop finely and set aside.

🐾 Heat the oil in a large skillet. Add the pork chops. Cook until browned; drain. Sprinkle the pork chops with seasoned salt; set aside.

🐾 Combine the soup, milk, sour cream, pepper and $^1/_2$ teaspoon seasoned salt in a large bowl and mix well. Stir in the potatoes, $^1/_2$ cup of the cheese, chopped onions and half the Onion Ringers.

🐾 Spoon the soup mixture into a 9x13-inch baking dish. Arrange the pork chops over the top.

🐾 Bake, covered, at 350 degrees for 35 to 40 minutes or until the pork chops are cooked through.

🐾 Top with the remaining $^1/_2$ cup cheese and Onion Ringers.

🐾 Bake for 5 minutes longer.

### GRAVIES

The cooking liquid that remains after you boil potatoes contains a lot of the potatoes' nutrients, so use it in making gravies or for moistening mashed potatoes. For a wonderful story about making gravy (and a terrific recipe), see "Grandma's Gravy," page 141.

# Parchment-Wrapped Potato Bundles

*Yield: 2 servings*

*6 ounces thinly sliced cooked*
*    lean ham*
*²/₃ pound (2 medium) russet*
*    potatoes, cut into ¹/₈-inch slices*
*1 small zucchini, cut into*
*    ¹/₄-inch slices*
*1 small crookneck squash, cut into*
*    ¹/₄-inch slices*
*1 small red bell pepper, cut into*
*    1-inch cubes*
*2 tablespoons lemon juice*
*1 teaspoon dried basil*
*¹/₄ teaspoon red pepper flakes*
*Salt and black pepper to taste*

🖎 Cut two 15-inch squares from kitchen parchment paper.

🖎 Place half the ham on a parchment square. Arrange half the potatoes in overlapping slices over the ham. Top with half the zucchini, squash and red pepper. Sprinkle with half the lemon juice, basil, red pepper flakes, salt and black pepper.

🖎 Fold 2 sides of the parchment over the filling in letter fashion. Grasp the 2 shorter open ends and pull up to meet. Fold down the open ends twice to seal. Repeat the process for the second bundle.

🖎 Place in a single layer in a shallow microwave-safe dish.

🖎 Microwave on High for 7 minutes. Rotate the bundles ¹/₂ turn. Microwave for 7 minutes longer.

🖎 Let stand for 3 minutes. If the potatoes are not tender, rewrap and Microwave on High briefly.

 ## EASY TURKEY SHEPHERD'S PIE

*Yield: 4 servings*

1 pound turkey cutlets, or 2 cups
    *chopped cooked turkey*
    *or chicken*
*Salt to taste*
*Pepper to taste*
*1 (10-ounce) can cream of*
    *mushroom soup*
*³/₄ cup skim milk*
*1 (10-ounce) package frozen mixed*
    *vegetables*
*2 tablespoons minced dried onions*
*¹/₂ teaspoon Italian seasoning*
    *or thyme*
*¹/₂ teaspoon salt*
*¹/₂ teaspoon pepper*
*8 servings prepared Ore-Ida frozen*
    *mashed potatoes (see Note)*

🖙 Sprinkle the cutlets lightly with salt and pepper. Sauté in a large nonstick skillet sprayed with nonstick cooking spray for 2 minutes per side or until cooked through. Remove from the skillet and cool slightly. Cut into ¹/₂-inch cubes.

🖙 Mix the soup and milk in a medium bowl. Stir in the mixed vegetables, onions, Italian seasoning, ¹/₂ teaspoon salt, ¹/₂ teaspoon pepper and turkey.

🖙 Spoon into four 1¹/₂x5-inch tart pans or potpie pans. Top with the mashed potatoes, smoothing to the edge. Place the pans on a large baking sheet.

🖙 Bake at 350 degrees for 25 to 30 minutes or until bubbly and lightly browned.

🖙

*Note: Prepare the mashed potatoes using 2²/₃ cups skim milk.*

🖙

## CHICKEN, HAM AND FENNEL POTPIES

These potpies are well worth the effort and can be made ahead.

*Yield: 8 potpies*

*2 small fennel bulbs*
*1³/₄ pounds boneless skinless*
*    chicken breast halves*
*5 cups canned low-salt*
*    chicken broth*
*¹/₂ cup diced carrot*
*1 (9-ounce) russet potato, cut into*
*    ¹/₂-inch cubes*
*5 tablespoons butter*
*5 tablespoons flour*
*2¹/₂ cups milk (not low-fat)*
*3 tablespoons fresh lemon juice*
*2 teaspoons fennel seeds*
*Salt to taste*
*4 ounces thinly sliced country ham,*
*    cut into julienne strips*
*Pepper to taste*
*Potpie Pastry*
*1 egg, beaten*

🐟 Trim the fennel bulbs. Cut lengthwise into quarters and discard the cores. Slice the fennel thinly.

🐟 Cut the chicken into 1-inch pieces.

🐟 Bring the broth to a boil in a Dutch oven over medium heat. Add the fennel. Cook for 7 minutes.

🐟 Add the chicken, carrot and potato. Simmer for 10 minutes or until the fennel, chicken and vegetables are tender. Pour into a strainer set over a bowl. Reserve the broth for other uses.

🐟 Melt the butter in a large heavy saucepan over medium-high heat. Add the flour. Cook for 2 minutes, stirring constantly. Stir in the milk gradually. Cook for 4 minutes or until the sauce thickens, whisking constantly. Add the lemon juice, fennel seeds and salt. Add the chicken mixture and ham and mix well. Season with salt and pepper. Pour into 8 individual ovenproof dishes or large custard cups. Cool completely.

🐟 Roll the pastry ¹/₈ inch thick on a floured surface. Cut out 8 rounds that measure ¹/₂ to 1 inch larger in diameter than the baking dishes. Use pastry scraps for decorative leaves if desired.

🐟 Lay 1 round over each dish. Press the overhang firmly to affix it to the side and top of the dish. Brush the bottom of the leaf cutouts with a small amount of water. Arrange over each potpie. Vent the tops to allow steam to escape. Place the dishes on a large baking sheet. Brush with the beaten egg.

🐟 Bake at 375 degrees for 40 minutes or until the potpies are heated through and the crusts are golden brown.

## Potpie Pastry

*3 cups sifted flour*
*¾ teaspoon salt*
*¾ cup chilled unsalted butter, cut
  into pieces*
*4½ tablespoons chilled shortening,
  cut into pieces*
*6 tablespoons (about) ice water*

🍃 Combine the flour and salt in a food processor container or blender container. Process until mixed.

🍃 Add the butter and shortening. Pulse until crumbly.

🍃 Add 4 tablespoons of the ice water. Process until mixed. Stir in the remaining water until the mixture forms moist clumps.

🍃 Shape the dough into a ball. Flatten into a disk.

🍃 Chill, wrapped in plastic wrap, for 1 to 24 hours.

### COOKING TIP

Beat an egg yolk or two instead of milk into mashed potatoes that will be used to top a casserole or shepherd's pie. This will help thicken the potatoes and keep them from spreading while baking.

## Roast Chicken with Olives and Potatoes

*Yield: 4 to 6 servings*

1 (7-pound) roasting chicken
6 tablespoons olive paste, divided
2 bay leaves
$1/4$ cup olive oil, divided
Salt and pepper to taste
$1/4$ cup fresh thyme leaves, divided
4 medium russet potatoes, peeled,
    cut into $1^1/_2$-inch pieces
2 tablespoons kalamata olives

🍃 Hold open the skin over the chicken breasts and legs. Rub 4 tablespoons of the olive paste over the breast and leg meat.

🍃 Spread the remaining 2 table-spoons olive paste inside the cavity of the chicken. Place the bay leaves in the cavity. Tie the legs together with string or secure with skewers. Rub 2 tablespoons of the olive oil over the outside of the chicken. Sprinkle with salt, pepper and 2 tablespoons of the thyme. Place in a large roasting pan.

🍃 Combine the potatoes, remaining 2 tablespoons olive oil, salt and pepper in a large bowl, tossing to coat. Sprinkle with the remaining 2 tablespoons thyme. Arrange the potatoes around the chicken in the pan.

🍃 Roast at 450 degrees for 15 minutes. Reduce the oven temperature to 375 degrees. Roast for 1 hour.

🍃 Add the olives to the pan. Roast for 10 minutes longer or until the chicken is cooked through and the juices run clear, basting occasionally with the pan drippings.

🍃 Place the chicken on a platter. Remove and discard the bay leaves. Surround with the potatoes and olives. Sprinkle with additional thyme.

🍃 Pour the pan drippings into a large cup and skim the top. Serve the pan drippings with the chicken.

# CRISPY POTATO CHICKEN

*Yield: 4 servings*

1 (8-ounce) russet potato, peeled,
    *coarsely shredded*
*3 to 4 tablespoons Dijon mustard*
*2 cloves of garlic, minced*
*2 whole chicken breasts (1 pound),*
    *skinned, split into halves*
*1 teaspoon olive oil*
*Freshly ground pepper to taste*
*Snipped fresh parsley, cilantro,*
    *rosemary or chives*

🐟 Place the potato in a bowl of ice water. Let stand for 5 minutes.

🐟 Combine the Dijon mustard and garlic in a bowl and mix well.

🐟 Spread the mustard mixture evenly over the meaty side of the chicken.

🐟 Place the chicken bone side down in a foil-lined 10x15-inch baking pan.

🐟 Drain the potato and pat dry with paper towels. Combine the potato and olive oil in a medium bowl, tossing to mix well.

🐟 Top each piece of chicken with $^1/_3$ cup of the potato mixture, forming a "skin." Sprinkle lightly with pepper.

🐟 Bake at 425 degrees for 45 to 50 minutes or until the chicken is cooked through and the potato is golden brown. May broil for 5 minutes to add additional browning.

🐟 Sprinkle with parsley, cilantro, rosemary, or chives, or other desired herbs.

# POTATO TURKEY TACOS

*Yield: 8 tacos*

12 ounces ground turkey (see Note)
2¹/₂ cups cubed frozen processed
    potatoes, thawed (see Note)
1 (10-ounce) can enchilada sauce
¹/₂ cup salsa
8 (7-inch) flour tortillas, or 8
    prepared crisp corn taco shells
¹/₂ cup shredded low-fat
    Cheddar cheese
³/₄ cup shredded iceberg lettuce
¹/₃ cup chopped tomato
2 tablespoons chopped red onion

🐚 Sauté the turkey in a nonstick skillet over medium heat until the turkey is cooked through.

🐚 Add the potatoes, enchilada sauce and salsa. Cook over medium heat for 4 to 5 minutes or until the potatoes are tender, stirring occasionally.

🐚 Place the tortillas in a sealable plastic bag, leaving one end open. Microwave on High for 1 minute. Remove the tortillas from the bag.

🐚 Spoon the turkey mixture onto the tortillas. Top with the cheese, lettuce, tomato and onion. Fold over and roll up.

🐚

*Note: May substitute ground beef for the turkey; may substitute diced cooked fresh russet potatoes for the frozen potatoes.*

🐚

# CRAB-STUFFED POTATOES

*Yield: 6 servings*

*3 large baking potatoes, scrubbed*
*¹/₄ cup melted butter*
*¹/₄ cup milk*
*¹/₄ teaspoon salt*
*¹/₄ teaspoon black pepper*
*¹/₂ bunch green onions*
*4 ounces canned lump crab meat*
*2 tablespoons mayonnaise*
*2 tablespoons sour cream*
*1 tablespoon lemon juice*
*¹/₈ teaspoon ground red pepper*
*6 slices bacon, crisp-fried, crumbled*

🖎 Bake the potatoes at 350 degrees for 1¹/₄ to 1¹/₂ hours or until tender.

🖎 Cut the potatoes into halves lengthwise. Scoop out the pulp, leaving a ¹/₄-inch shell.

🖎 Beat the potato pulp in a bowl until mashed. Beat in the butter, milk, salt and black pepper.

🖎 Slice the white part of the green onions into the potato mixture. Reserve the green tops.

🖎 Spoon the potato mixture into the shells. Place on baking sheets.

🖎 Combine the crab meat, mayonnaise, sour cream, lemon juice and red pepper in a small bowl and mix well. Mound onto the stuffed potatoes. Press the bacon onto the top of the potatoes.

🖎 Bake at 350 degrees for 40 to 45 minutes or until heated through.

🖎 Slice the reserved green onion tops. Sprinkle over the potatoes.

# POTATO-CRUSTED HALIBUT STEAKS

*Yield: 6 servings*

## Sauce

*1 cup dry white wine*
*1 large shallot, chopped*
*1 tablespoon fresh lemon juice*
*1 tablespoon Worcestershire sauce*
*1/2 cup chopped parsley*
*1/2 cup extra-virgin olive oil*
*Salt and pepper to taste*
*1/4 cup mayonnaise*
*1 tablespoon capers, drained*
*4 flat anchovies, chopped*

*6 (7 ounces each) boneless halibut*
*    steaks, 1 inch thick*
*12 ounces russet potatoes, peeled,*
*    coarsely grated (see Note)*
*2 tablespoons (or more) olive oil*
*Salt and pepper to taste*

Oil a shallow baking pan lightly.

For the sauce, boil the white wine with the shallot until the liquid is reduced to 1/2 cup. Remove from the heat. Whisk in the lemon juice, Worcestershire sauce and parsley. Add 1/2 cup olive oil in a stream, whisking until well mixed. Season with salt and pepper. Set aside and keep warm.

Mix the mayonnaise, capers, anchovies, salt and pepper in a bowl.

Pat the steaks dry. Season with salt and pepper. Spread the mayonnaise mixture evenly over the steaks.

Sprinkle a heaping 1/4 cup of the potatoes evenly over the mayonnaise mixture.

Heat 2 tablespoons olive oil in a nonstick skillet over moderate heat. Add 2 of the steaks potato side down. Cook for 5 minutes or until the potatoes are golden brown and cooked through, pressing the steaks down with a slotted spatula occasionally.

Invert the steaks into the prepared baking pan. Season with salt and pepper. Repeat the procedure with the remaining steaks, adding additional olive oil to the skillet if needed.

Bake the steaks on the middle oven rack at 400 degrees for 10 to 15 minutes or just until cooked through.

Serve immediately with the sauce.

*Note: May substitute thawed and dried frozen hash browns for the russet potatoes.*

## Stuffed Boneless Brook Trout

From *Bound to Please*,
Junior League of Boise, 1983

*Yield: 2 servings*

¹/₂ cup chopped fresh mushrooms
1¹/₂ cups diced red potatoes
1 teaspoon chopped shallots
1 teaspoon chopped chives
¹/₂ cup plum tomatoes,
   chopped, seeded
¹/₄ cup butter
1 tablespoon flour
¹/₄ cup milk
1 teaspoon salt
¹/₈ teaspoon pepper
3 tablespoons dry white wine
1 cup crab meat
1 teaspoon lemon juice
2 (10 ounces each) rainbow trout,
   cleaned, boned

 Sauté the mushrooms, potatoes, shallots, chives and tomatoes in the butter in a large skillet until tender. Blend in the flour. Add the milk, salt and pepper. Cook until thickened and bubbly, stirring constantly. Stir in the wine. Add the crab meat and lemon juice.

 Stuff each trout with half the mixture. Broil, wrapped in foil, for 5 minutes per side.

 May also be grilled over low heat for 10 minutes per side.

## Pesto Salmon with Pan-Roasted Potatoes

*Yield: 2 servings*

²/₃ pound (2 medium) potatoes, cut
   into 1-inch chunks
2 (6 to 8 ounces each) salmon
   steaks
2 tablespoons prepared pesto,
   thawed if frozen
1 tablespoon olive oil
2 cloves of garlic, minced
Salt and pepper to taste

 Place the potatoes in a shallow 1-quart microwave-safe dish. Cover with plastic wrap and vent 1 corner. Microwave on High for 6 minutes or just until tender.

 Spread each steak evenly with the pesto. Place on a rimmed baking sheet. Bake at 400 degrees for 15 to 20 minutes or until the salmon is opaque throughout.

 Combine the olive oil and garlic in a medium nonstick skillet over high heat. Add the potatoes. Pan-roast for 5 to 8 minutes or until golden brown, tossing frequently. Season with salt and pepper.

 Serve the potatoes with the salmon.

# RACLETTE

A traditional country dish of
melted cheese, made in many
parts of Switzerland and France.
The word raclette comes from the
French racler, meaning to scrape.

*Yield: 8 servings*

*40 small red potatoes*
*3 pounds raclette, fontina, Muenster,*
   *Tilsit or Monterey Jack cheese*
   *(about 6 ounces per serving)*
*Cornichons (small tart sour pickles)*
   *or gherkins*
*Pickled onions*
*Freshly ground black pepper*

☞ Boil the potatoes in water to
cover in a saucepan until tender
but not mushy; drain. Set aside and
keep warm.

☞ Build a hot fire in a fireplace.

☞ Warm 8 heatproof plates in a
200-degree oven.

☞ Have at hand an oven mitt, wide
tongs and a large knife.

☞ Wearing the oven mitt and using
tongs, hold the cheese on edge next to
the fire, keeping the cut side vertical
and perpendicular to the flames. When
the cheese begins to bubble and melt,
use the knife to quickly scrape 1
portion onto a heated plate.

☞ Serve immediately with the
potatoes, cornichons and pickled
onions. Sprinkle with pepper.

☞ Repeat the scraping 1 serving at a
time as often as needed.

☞ Serve with white wine and beer.

☞

*Note: An alternative method
of preparation is to place 2 to
3 paper-thin slices of cheese
(1 serving) on a metal or other
ovenproof plate. Place in a
450-degree oven until the cheese
is melted. Serve immediately
with the potatoes, cornichons,
pickled onions and pepper.*

☞

# OLD-WORLD VEGETABLE CASSEROLE

*Yield: 4 to 6 servings*

4 medium russet potatoes, cut into
    small pieces
1¹/₂ cups chopped onions
3 tablespoons butter
4 cups packed shredded
    green cabbage
¹/₂ teaspoon ground caraway seeds
1 teaspoon salt
1¹/₂ cups cottage cheese
¹/₂ cup sour cream
¹/₂ cup plain yogurt
¹/₂ teaspoon dillweed
2 tablespoons cider vinegar
¹/₄ cup sunflower kernels, divided
Pepper to taste
Paprika to taste

🖝 Boil the potatoes in water to cover in a saucepan until very tender. Set aside and keep warm.

🖝 Sauté the onions in the butter in a saucepan for 5 minutes. Add the cabbage, caraway seeds and salt. Sauté until the cabbage is tender.

🖝 Drain the potatoes. Mash with the cottage cheese, sour cream and yogurt.

🖝 Combine the potato mixture and cabbage mixture in a large bowl and mix well. Add the dillweed, vinegar, 2 tablespoons of the sunflower kernels and pepper. Adjust the seasonings.

🖝 Spread in a buttered deep 2-quart casserole. Sprinkle with the paprika and remaining 2 tablespoons sunflower kernels.

🖝 Bake at 350 degrees for 35 to 40 minutes or until heated through.

If your potatoes are a
little old, you can
improve their flavor by
adding a little sugar to
the boiling water.

# FEISTY RED POTATO FAJITAS

*Yield: 2 servings*

*6 small red potatoes*

## Bean Salsa
*1 cup canned black beans, drained*
*1 cup prepared tomato salsa*

## Marinade
*2 tablespoons lime juice*
*2 tablespoons olive oil*
*1 tablespoon minced jalapeño*
*2 teaspoons ground cumin*
*1 green bell pepper, thinly sliced*
*1 onion, thinly sliced*

*4 (8-inch) flour tortillas*

🐟 Parboil the potatoes for 12 minutes; drain. Cut into 1/4-inch French-fry-style pieces and set aside.

🐟 For the salsa, mix the beans and tomato salsa in a medium bowl. Set aside.

🐟 For the marinade, combine the lime juice, olive oil, jalapeño and cumin in a large bowl. Add the green pepper, onion and potatoes and toss to coat. Marinate for 30 minutes.

🐟 Remove the green pepper, onion and potatoes from the marinade. May reserve the marinade for occasional basting during cooking.

🐟 Cook the marinated vegetables on a very hot cast-iron griddle or grill until of desired crispness.

🐟 Sprinkle the tortillas lightly with water. Heat 1 at a time in a skillet very briefly until pliable.

🐟 Spoon 1/4 of the vegetable filling and 1/4 of the salsa onto each tortilla and roll up. Serve immediately.

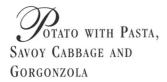

# Potato with Pasta, Savoy Cabbage and Gorgonzola

*Yield: 4 servings*

10 ounces orecchiette (little ear-
    shaped pasta), about 2²/₃ cups
1 (8-ounce) russet potato, peeled,
    cut into ¹/₂-inch cubes
4 cups packed ¹/₂-inch strips savoy
    cabbage, about 8 ounces
3 tablespoons butter
2 tablespoons olive oil
3 large cloves of garlic,
    finely chopped
6 fresh sage leaves
5 ounces Gorgonzola cheese,
    crumbled, divided
Salt and pepper to taste

🖜 Cook the pasta in boiling salted water in a large saucepan until al dente. Drain in a colander set over another large saucepan, reserving the cooking liquid. Rinse the pasta under cold running water.

🖜 Return the reserved cooking liquid to a boil. Add the potato. Cook for 7 minutes or just until tender.

🖜 Add the pasta and cabbage. Cook for 1 minute or until the cabbage wilts, stirring constantly.

🖜 Heat the butter and olive oil in a heavy skillet over medium-low heat until the butter melts. Add the garlic and sage. Sauté for 1 minute.

🖜 Drain the pasta mixture, reserving ¹/₂ cup cooking liquid.

🖜 Add the pasta mixture and reserved cooking liquid to the garlic mixture. Add 1¹/₄ cups of the cheese, tossing until the cheese is melted. Season with salt and pepper.

🖜 Spoon into a 9x13-inch glass baking dish. Top with the remaining cheese.

🖜 Bake at 400 degrees for 5 minutes or until the cheese on top is melted.

# Gnocchi Primavera

*Yield: 4 to 6 servings*

## Gnocchi (dumplings)

*3 to 4 medium russet potatoes*
 *(about 1 to 1¹/₂ pounds)*
*1 teaspoon salt*
*1¹/₂ cups flour*
*1 tablespoon olive oil*
*2 eggs, lightly beaten*
*3 quarts water*
*2 tablespoons butter, chopped*

## Sauce

*4 ounces fresh asparagus, cut into*
 *2-inch pieces*
*2 tablespoons olive oil*
*4 shallots or green onions, minced*
*1 clove of garlic, minced*
*2 ounces snow peas or sugar snap*
 *peas, strings removed*
*2 zucchini, sliced diagonally*
*4 ounces green beans, cut into*
 *2-inch pieces*
*2 tablespoons chopped fresh basil*
*¹/₄ cup chopped fresh parsley*
*12 cherry tomatoes, cut into halves*
*Pepper to taste*
*¹/₂ cup grated Parmesan cheese*

For the gnocchi, boil the potatoes in water to cover in a saucepan until tender; drain well. Let stand until cool enough to handle; peel.

Force the potatoes through a potato ricer or push through a sieve with the back of a wooden spoon. Measure out 3 cups. Reserve the remaining potatoes for another use.

Combine the potatoes, 1 teaspoon salt, flour, 1 tablespoon olive oil and eggs in a bowl, stirring until a thick dough forms.

Turn the dough onto a floured board. Knead 15 times. Roll into ¹/₂-inch ropes, using ¹/₂ cup of dough at a time. Cut each into 1¹/₄-inch pieces.

Place each piece of dough near the tines of a floured fork. Press the center of each piece of dough with a finger and roll the dumpling toward you, allowing the tines to make decorative ridges (see Note). Place on a generously floured baking sheet.

Bring 3 quarts lightly salted oiled water to a rapid boil in a large saucepan. Add ¹/₃ of the gnocchi. Reduce the heat until the water is just boiling. Cook for 5 minutes after the dumplings bob to the surface of the water. Drain and toss with the butter. Keep warm in a 200-degree oven while cooking the remaining gnocchi.

For the sauce, boil the asparagus in water to cover in a saucepan for 5 minutes; drain well.

Heat 2 tablespoons olive oil in a large skillet. Add the shallots, garlic, asparagus, snow peas, zucchini and green beans. Steam, covered, for 5 minutes. Stir to mix well. Add the basil and parsley. Cook, covered, until the vegetables are tender-crisp.

Stir in the tomatoes at serving time. Season with salt and pepper.

Toss the gnocchi with the sauce. Sprinkle with the cheese.

*Note: A simpler shaping for gnocchi requires only that each be rolled lightly in the center with a floured forefinger to give it a bow shape. Although the dough should be used as soon as possible after it is made to prevent it from becoming too soft to handle, gnocchi can be cooked and kept warm for several hours.*

 ## Main-Dish
### Baked Potatoes

*Yield: 4 servings*

*4 large russet potatoes*

☞ Scrub the potatoes. Bake at 425 degrees for 45 to 60 minutes or until tender. Do not pierce, cut or wrap in foil. "Blossom" the potato as described on page 136.

 ## Taco-Topped Bakers

*Yield: 4 servings*

*1 pound ground beef*
*¹/₂ cup chopped onion*
*1 (4-ounce) can diced green chiles*
*1 cup taco sauce*
*¹/₂ cup water*
*1 teaspoon cumin*
*1 teaspoon chili powder*
*¹/₂ teaspoon paprika*
*¹/₂ teaspoon garlic salt*
*4 large russet potatoes, freshly baked*
*2 cups shredded Cheddar cheese*
*1 cup sour cream*
*1 tomato, chopped*

☞ Brown the ground beef in a large skillet, stirring until crumbly. Drain in a colander and rinse with hot water to reduce fat. Return the ground beef to the skillet.

☞ Add the onion, green chiles, taco sauce, water, cumin, chili powder, paprika and garlic salt. Simmer for 20 minutes, stirring occasionally.

☞ Blossom and fluff the potatoes (see page 136). Spoon the ground beef mixture over the potatoes. Top with the cheese, sour cream and tomato.

 ## Reuben-Topped Bakers

*Yield: 4 servings*

*2 cups shredded cooked corned beef*
*2 cups sauerkraut, drained*
*1 cup shredded Swiss cheese*
*1 teaspoon caraway seeds*
*4 large russet potatoes, freshly baked*
*¹/₄ cup crumbled crisp-fried bacon*

☞ Mix the corned beef, sauerkraut, cheese and caraway seeds in a bowl. Blossom and fluff the potatoes (see page 136). Spoon the corned beef mixture over the potatoes.

☞ Broil for 5 minutes or until the topping is heated through and the cheese begins to melt. Remove from the oven. Sprinkle with the bacon.

# STROGANOFF-TOPPED BAKERS

*Yield: 4 servings*

1 pound ground beef
$^1/_2$ cup minced onion
1 clove of garlic, minced
2 tablespoons flour
1 teaspoon salt
$^1/_4$ teaspoon pepper
8 ounces mushrooms, sliced
1 (10-ounce) can cream of
    mushroom soup
1 cup sour cream
4 large russet potatoes, freshly baked
2 tablespoons minced fresh parsley

🖝 Brown the ground beef in a large skillet over medium heat, stirring until crumbly; drain and rinse with warm water to remove excess fat. Return the ground beef to the skillet.

🖝 Add the onion and garlic. Sauté for 3 minutes.

🖝 Stir in the flour, salt, pepper and mushrooms. Cook for 5 minutes.

🖝 Add the soup. Simmer for 10 minutes. Stir in the sour cream.

🖝 Blossom and fluff the potatoes. Spoon the ground beef mixture over the potatoes.

🖝 Sprinkle with the parsley.

# 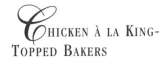CHICKEN À LA KING-TOPPED BAKERS

*Yield: 4 servings*

6 tablespoons butter or margarine
6 tablespoons flour
3 cups chicken stock or low-sodium
    chicken broth
2 egg yolks, beaten
2 cups chopped cooked chicken
    (see Note)
1 cup chopped mushrooms
$^1/_2$ cup chopped pimentos
Salt and pepper to taste
$^1/_2$ cup blanched slivered almonds
2 tablespoons dry sherry
4 large russet potatoes, freshly baked
Paprika to taste

🐟 Melt the butter in a large skillet. Stir in the flour. Cook until bubbly, stirring constantly. Remove from the heat.

🐟 Add the chicken stock. Return to the heat. Cook until the mixture is thickened and has come to a gentle boil. Reduce the heat to medium-low.

🐟 Stir $^1/_2$ cup of the hot mixture into the egg yolks; stir the egg yolks into the hot mixture.

🐟 Add the chicken, mushrooms and pimentos. Season with salt and pepper. Stir in the almonds and sherry.

🐟 Blossom and fluff the potatoes. Spoon the chicken mixture over the potatoes. Sprinkle with paprika.

🐟

*Note: May substitute chopped cooked turkey or tuna for the chicken.*

🐟

## QUICK TOPPERS

For a quick meal, top baked potatoes with shredded cooked chicken, minced red onion and red bell pepper, mashed avocado, and garlic; chopped tomato, rosemary, toasted walnuts, and freshly grated Parmesan cheese; minced leeks, smoked salmon, snipped fresh dill, and plain yogurt; or pepperoni, mushroom, and olive slices, pizza sauce, and shredded mozzarella cheese.

# Side DISHES

## GRANDMA'S GRAVY

While meeting with the minister to discuss my grandmother's funeral, we cousins started talking about what we remembered the most about Grandma. We all had one common memory: her good gravy and the ceremony surrounding its creation.

As a young child, I often spent days at Grandma's farm. Before I was to visit, Grandma would call me and ask me what I wanted for dinner. My reply was always the same, "Fried chicken, mashed potatoes, gravy, and creamed corn." The key to the meal was Grandma's gravy, and for me, the chance to participate in its making.

Being near Grandma in her kitchen while she was cooking was always special. Grandma did not have to call me to come into the kitchen because from any part of the house or yard I would smell the aroma of chicken frying. The aroma that signaled that the time to make the gravy had arrived. Once in the kitchen, Grandma would invite me to the place of honor, the stool by the stove, where she would let me help her make the gravy.

Grandma would open the lid of her electric skillet, probably one of the first ever made, where I would see the crispy chicken. She would then remove the chicken to a warming tray, leaving all of the crispies (as she would call them) and drippings in the pan. She always cautioned, "Don't eat the crispies because they give the gravy its flavor."

Grandma would hand me the slotted spoon as if it were a scepter. In my eyes, as a young child, it was the spoon that gave me the power to make the greatest gravy. Sitting next to Grandma I would stir and dislodge all those wonderful crispies from the bottom of the pan. If there wasn't enough grease, Grandma would add a little bit more from her reserve, and I would stir until it melted. Grandma then would sprinkle in the flour while I continued to stir to make sure the flour absorbed the grease evenly with no lumps or burning. Grandma lovingly commanded, "Keep stirring, so you don't burn the flour." She would pour in whole milk until the base started forming a thick and creamy gravy.

At this point, Grandma would go mash the potatoes. I was charged with keeping the gravy from scorching and getting too thick. If it seemed to thicken too fast, I would call Grandma so she could pour in some water from her tea kettle, which would always help.

As soon as Grandma turned her back, the spoon would go from the gravy and then into my mouth. I would load it, of course, with some of those crispies. At that age, I believed she never knew I took a bite; however, now having my own children, I know a certain look on children's faces gives them away. Plus, I count every crispy!

I would continue stirring the gravy while Grandma would put the rest of the meal on the table. Keeping the gravy hot was of foremost importance to Grandma; therefore, it would be the last item brought to the table, but not before Grandma had tasted and seasoned the gravy. When it met with her approval, she would praise me for my work, saying, "I couldn't have done it without you." Dismissed from my stool, I would run to the table with pride and anticipation of a great dinner to come.

Looking back, I rarely saw my grandma sit down. She was always working in the kitchen. As she got older, she acquired Alzheimer's, and her disease robbed her and my family of many gifts like the times spent in her kitchen. Over the years, trying to recapture those special moments, I decided I would try to make Grandma's fried chicken, mashed potatoes, gravy, and creamed corn. I tried it, and it didn't work — the dinner did not taste the same. I decided it must have been that slotted spoon, and I rushed right out and bought one just like Grandma's and tried to make the dinner again. It still did not taste quite right.

Not until remembering Grandma with my cousins did I discover that we had all tried to recreate Grandma's gravy, but, of course, with no luck! I disclosed to them that I had even gone out and bought a slotted spoon, thinking it would make the difference.

We then decided that it was the time spent with Grandma in her kitchen that had made the food so good. Having come to that conclusion, my slotted spoon found a new home: in my children's sandbox.

*— by Marie Johnson*

# GRANDMA'S GRAVY

*Yield: 1 cup*

*Reserved crispies from cooked meat*
*2 tablespoons hot pan drippings*
*2 tablespoons flour*
*1 cup milk or potato water*
 *(reserved from boiled potatoes)*
*Salt and pepper*
*Preferred herbs*

🖛 Remove the meat to a warm platter, reserving the meat crispies and pan drippings.

🖛 Whisk flour into the pan drippings. Stir to make a thick paste, taking care not to burn the flour.

🖛 Slowly add the milk or potato water, stirring constantly until the gravy thickens. Add more milk or potato water if you like thinner gravy.

🖛 Season with salt, pepper and other favorite herbs.

🖛 Serve hot with mashed potatoes and favorite memories of Grandma.

## Potato Pear Tart

From Helcia Graf, *Hungarian Radish in Sun Valley*

*Yield: 8 servings*

*1 unbaked tart shell*
*Sauce*
*10 (2 ounces each) new potatoes,*
*    cut into 1/8-inch slices*
*3 (8 ounces each) Anjou pears*

### Sauce
*1/2 cup chopped leeks*
*2 tablespoons dry white wine*
*2 cups whipping cream*
*1/4 cup grated Romano cheese*
*Salt and pepper to taste*

🖋 Fit the tart shell into a 10-inch tart pan. Bake using the package directions. Let cool.

🖋 For the sauce, combine the leeks, wine and whipping cream in a medium saucepan. Bring to a gentle boil over medium-high heat, stirring constantly. Cook until reduced to 1 1/2 cups, stirring constantly.

🖋 Stir the cheese, salt and pepper into the sauce. Pour into a small bowl. Cover with plastic wrap, pressing the plastic directly onto the surface of the sauce. Chill thoroughly.

🖋 Arrange 1/3 of the potato slices in the tart shell so that the slices overlap slightly. Spoon 1/4 of the sauce over the potatoes. Repeat layers twice.

🖋 Peel the pears and cut into halves lengthwise. Remove the seeds and cores. Cut each half crosswise into 1/4-inch slices. Arrange the slices spoke-fashion over the potatoes, fanning out the slices slightly.

🖋 Spoon the remaining sauce over the pears, coating the pears completely.

🖋 Place the tart on a baking sheet. Bake at 350 degrees for 1 hour or until the potatoes in the center are tender.

🖋 Cool on a wire rack for 20 minutes. Cut into wedges to serve.

🖋

*This tart is perfect for a late New Year's Eve celebration with a selection of hard cheeses, crackers, dark chocolates and Champagne.*

🖋

## CREAMY HERBED POTATOES

*Yield: 6 to 8 servings*

2 cups whipping cream (see Note)
1 (4-ounce) package Rondele cheese
   with herbs, softened (see Note)
3 pounds red new potatoes,
   thinly sliced
Salt and pepper to taste
1½ tablespoons chopped
   fresh parsley

☞ Combine the whipping cream and cheese in a saucepan. Heat over medium heat until blended and smooth, stirring constantly.

☞ Arrange half the potatoes in overlapping rows in a greased 9x13-inch baking dish. Season generously with salt and pepper.

☞ Pour half the cheese mixture over the potatoes.

☞ Repeat the layers with the potatoes and the cheese mixture.

☞ Bake at 400 degrees for 1 hour or until the top is golden brown and the potatoes are tender.

☞ Sprinkle with the parsley.

☞

*Note: To reduce fat, substitute evaporated skim milk for the whipping cream. The cheese may be any herbed cream cheese of your choice.*

☞

## CHEESY POTATO CASSEROLE

*Yield: 8 servings*

1 (10-ounce) can cream of chicken
    soup (see Note)
2 cups sour cream or low-fat
    sour cream
1½ teaspoons salt
¼ teaspoon pepper
3 green onions, chopped
2 cups shredded Cheddar cheese
1 (32-ounce) package frozen
    hash brown potatoes

### Topping
¼ cup melted butter or margarine
2 cups crushed cornflakes

🖝 Combine the soup, sour cream, salt, pepper, green onions and cheese in a large bowl and mix well. Add the potatoes and mix well.

🖝 Spoon into a greased 9x13-inch baking pan.

🖝 Top with a mixture of the butter and cornflakes.

🖝 Bake at 350 degrees for 45 minutes or until bubbly around the edges.

🖝 May sprinkle with 3 tablespoons sesame seeds and paprika to taste instead of topping with the cornflake mixture.

🖝 Easy and delicious accompaniment to ham, turkey or chicken dinners.

🖝

*Note: You may substitute cream of mushroom or cream of celery soup for a different flavor.*

🖝

## POTATOES AND BROTH

From John Mortimer, owner and chef, B.B. Strand's

*Yield: 6 servings*

*4 large russet potatoes*
*1 tablespoon butter*
*1 teaspoon finely minced garlic*
*¹/₂ red onion, cut into julienne slices*
*1 rib celery, cut diagonally into*
  *thin slices*
*¹/₂ red bell pepper (about ¹/₂ cup),*
  *cut into julienne slices*
*1¹/₂ cups chicken stock*
*1 teaspoon thyme*
*¹/₂ teaspoon ground rosemary*
*¹/₂ teaspoon crumbled sage*
*1 teaspoon salt*
*¹/₂ teaspoon ground pepper*

☛ Bake the potatoes at 425 degrees for 1 hour. Let cool. Peel and cut into cubes.

☛ Melt the butter in a large ovenproof skillet over medium heat.

☛ Add the garlic, onion, celery and red pepper. Sauté until the onion is translucent.

☛ Add the chicken stock and potatoes. Bring to a boil.

☛ Add the thyme, rosemary, sage, salt and pepper and mix well.

☛ Bake at 350 degrees for 45 minutes.

☛ Serve with a slotted spoon to allow some of the broth to fall off the potatoes.

## POTATO TRIVIA

The potato is the first item tasted from a person's plate.

# TURKEY DRESSING

*Yield: Dressing for*
*1 (15- to 18-pound) turkey*
*(see Note)*

*Turkey giblets and neck*
*2 teaspoons salt*
*1 large onion, finely chopped*
*6 cups seasoned bread crumbs or*
*    bread cubes*
*1 cup warm water*
*¹/₃ cup butter*
*6 medium potatoes, peeled, boiled,*
*    crushed into chunks*
*Salt to taste*

🖎 Combine the giblets, neck, 2 teaspoons salt and water to cover in a saucepan. Boil for 25 minutes. Drain, reserving the cooking liquid. Let the meat cool slightly.

🖎 Remove the meat from the neck. Process the neck meat, giblets and onion in a meat grinder or food processor.

🖎 Combine the bread crumbs and warm water in a medium bowl. If using bread cubes, stir until crumbly.

🖎 Combine the butter, reserved cooking liquid, meat mixture, bread crumbs and potatoes in a large bowl. Add additional water if needed. Season with salt to taste.

🖎 For superior texture and to avoid the danger of spoilage, dressing should be prepared just before cooking the turkey. Stuff the turkey lightly or bake the dressing separately in a greased pan at 325 degrees for 45 to 55 minutes (see Note).

🖎 If there is leftover dressing after serving, remove it promptly from the turkey cavity and refrigerate it separately.

🖎

*Note: A useful rule of thumb in judging the amount of stuffing needed is to allow ¹/₂ cup stuffing per each pound of turkey. Dressings are done when they reach an internal temperature of 165 to 170 degrees.*

🖎

# ROASTED POTATO FANS

*Yield: 4 servings*

4 medium Idaho russet potatoes
1 teaspoon salt
3 tablespoons melted butter or
  margarine
2 tablespoons chopped fresh herbs
  such as parsley, chives, thyme,
  rosemary or sage, or
  2 to 3 teaspoons dried herbs
$^1/_4$ cup shredded Cheddar cheese
2 tablespoons grated
  Parmesan cheese

🖝 Peel the potatoes. Make slits in the potatoes at $^1/_4$- to $^1/_8$-inch intervals, taking care not to cut all the way through the potatoes; leave approximately a $^1/_2$-inch uncut base on each potato.

🖝 Place the potatoes in a lightly greased baking dish. Fan them slightly.

🖝 Sprinkle with the salt. Drizzle with the butter. Sprinkle with the herbs.

🖝 Bake at 425 degrees for 50 minutes.

🖝 Remove from the oven. Sprinkle with Cheddar cheese and Parmesan cheese.

🖝 Bake for 10 to 15 minutes longer or until the cheeses are melted and the top is lightly browned.

## POTATO TRIVIA

Potatoes come in

colors of purple,

yellow, red, and brown.

## "Smoke Stacked" Potatoes

From Chef Lou Aaron, Westside
Catering Company, Boise, Idaho

*Yield: 4 servings*

3 russet potatoes, about 1¼ pounds
1½ cups ricotta cheese
½ teaspoon liquid smoke
2 eggs
½ teaspoon pepper
¾ cup chopped green onions
Grated zest of 1 lemon
¾ cup shredded mozzarella cheese
¾ cup shredded Cheddar cheese

### Garnish
*Sour cream or plain yogurt*

🐦 Combine the potatoes with water
to cover in a medium saucepan. Cook,
covered, for 20 to 25 minutes or until
the potatoes are tender; drain. Slice
the potatoes thinly.

🐦 Combine the ricotta cheese, liquid
smoke, eggs and pepper in a blender
container or food processor container.
Process for 10 seconds.

🐦 Coat a 9-inch pie plate with
nonstick cooking spray. Layer ⅓ of
the potatoes, half the egg mixture,
⅓ of the green onions, ⅓ of the
lemon zest, half the mozzarella cheese,
half the Cheddar cheese, ⅓ of the
potatoes and the remaining egg
mixture, potatoes, green onions,
lemon zest, mozzarella cheese and
Cheddar cheese in the pie plate.

🐦 Bake at 375 degrees for 30 to 40
minutes or until golden brown.

🐦 Garnish with sour cream or
yogurt.

🐦

*Note: This dish may be prepared
with reduced-fat cheeses. The
potatoes may be used peeled or
unpeeled.*

🐦

 RATATOUILLE

*Yield: 8 servings*

1 eggplant, peeled, cut into cubes
1 large russet potato, cut into cubes
    (see Note)
2 zucchini, cut into cubes
1 onion, cut into cubes
2 green bell peppers, cut into cubes
1 carrot, cut into cubes
2 tablespoons chopped parsley
$^1/_2$ cup olive oil, divided
1 tablespoon salt
2 teaspoons Tabasco sauce
1 teaspoon pepper
4 tomatoes, chopped or sliced
$^1/_2$ cup uncooked rice (not instant)
2 tablespoons wine vinegar
$^1/_2$ cup water
2 cups shredded Monterey Jack
    cheese

🖝 Combine the eggplant, potato, zucchini, onion, green peppers and carrot in a large bowl and mix well.

🖝 Mix the parsley, $^1/_4$ cup of the olive oil, salt, Tabasco sauce and pepper in a small bowl. Pour over the vegetable mixture and toss to coat.

🖝 Grease the bottom, sides and top edge of a 2-quart casserole. Layer half the tomatoes in the prepared casserole. Layer half the vegetable mixture over the tomatoes. Sprinkle with the rice. Layer the remaining vegetable mixture and remaining tomatoes over the rice.

🖝 Mix the remaining $^1/_4$ cup olive oil, wine vinegar and water in a small bowl. Pour over the vegetables.

🖝 Bake, covered, at 350 degrees for $1^1/_2$ hours. Remove the cover. Sprinkle with the cheese. Bake, uncovered, for 30 minutes.

🖝 This hearty dish is perfect for the Dutch oven, at home or at camp.

🖝

*Note: The potato may be used peeled or unpeeled.*

🖝

# Tomatoes Stuffed with Duchesse Potatoes

*Yield: 6 servings*

6 medium russet potatoes, peeled,
   cut into cubes
1 teaspoon salt
$^1/_8$ teaspoon white pepper
$^1/_4$ cup chopped green onions
$^1/_4$ teaspoon nutmeg
2 eggs
2 egg yolks
6 medium tomatoes
Salt to taste
Black pepper to taste
$^1/_4$ cup grated Parmesan cheese
2 tablespoons melted butter

### Garnish
*Sprigs of fresh parsley*

🖙 Combine the potatoes, 1 teaspoon salt and water to cover in a saucepan. Boil until tender; drain.

🖙 Place the potatoes in a medium bowl. Mash with a mixer at low speed or by hand.

🖙 Add $^1/_8$ teaspoon white pepper, green onions and nutmeg.

🖙 Beat the eggs and egg yolks in a small bowl until foamy. Add to the potatoes and whip until fluffy.

🖙 Cut small slices from the bottoms of the tomatoes so that they sit flat. Cut off the top third of the tomatoes with a zigzag cut.

🖙 Scoop out the centers of the tomatoes. Sprinkle lightly with salt and black pepper to taste. Invert onto a tray to drain.

🖙 Fill a cookie press or pastry bag fitted with a decorative tip with the potato mixture. Pipe into the tomatoes, heaping over the tops.

🖙 Sprinkle with the cheese. Brush with the butter.

🖙 Place on a baking sheet. Bake at 450 degrees for 5 to 10 minutes or until browned.

🖙 Garnish with parsley.

🖙 Perfect for serving when entertaining, these tomatoes may be prepared and refrigerated up to 4 hours in advance. To reheat, bake at 350 degrees for 20 to 25 minutes. Then increase the oven temperature to 450 degrees for browning.

# POTATOES IN A PASTRY SHELL

*Yield: 6 to 8 servings*

*4 cups cooked hot or cold potato*
*pulp (see Note)*
*¹/₃ cup melted butter or margarine*
*¹/₄ cup whipping cream, heated*
*¹/₂ cup finely chopped parsley*
*3 cloves of garlic, minced or pressed*
*1 teaspoon Italian seasoning*
*Salt and pepper to taste*
*4 frozen puff pastry shells, thawed*
*1 egg, lightly beaten*

🐚 Combine the potato pulp, butter, whipping cream, parsley, garlic and Italian seasoning in a large bowl. Blend gently with a fork without mashing. Season with salt and pepper.

🐚 Stack 2 pastry shells together. Roll into a 9¹/₂-inch round on a floured board. Place on a 10x15-inch baking sheet.

🐚 Stack the remaining 2 shells together. Roll into a 10¹/₂-inch round on a floured board.

🐚 Mound the potatoes on the smaller round, leaving a ¹/₂-inch border. Top with the larger round, pressing the edges together firmly to seal. Fold the bottom edge over the top edge, pressing firmly with fingers or a fork to seal tightly. Pat the top to flatten.

🐚 Brush the egg over the pastry. Make 3 slashes in the top of the pastry.

🐚 Place the baking sheet on the lowest oven rack. Bake at 400 degrees for 25 minutes or until golden brown.

🐚 Remove to a serving platter with a wide spatula. Cut into wedges.

🐚

*Note: Five medium baked russet potatoes should yield about 4 cups pulp.*

🐚

# COTTAGE MUSHROOM POTATO BAKE

*Yield: 10 servings*

8 medium potatoes, peeled
2 large onions, sliced
$1/4$ cup butter, divided
1 pound fresh mushrooms,
    cleaned, sliced
2 cups small curd cottage cheese
2 cups sour cream
2 teaspoons salt
2 teaspoons pepper
2 teaspoons dried thyme
2 cups shredded sharp
    Cheddar cheese

🖋 Boil the potatoes in water to cover in a saucepan just until tender; drain. Cut into $1/8$-inch slices and set aside.

🖋 Sauté the onions in 2 tablespoons of the butter in a skillet. Remove the onions and set aside.

🖋 Sauté the mushrooms in the remaining 2 tablespoons butter in a skillet. Set aside.

🖋 Mix the cottage cheese and sour cream in a small bowl.

🖋 Layer the potatoes, onions, mushrooms and cottage cheese mixture in a greased 9x13-inch baking dish, sprinkling each layer with the salt, pepper and thyme.

🖋 Top with the cheese.

🖋 Bake, covered, at 350 degrees for 20 minutes.

🖋 May be prepared and refrigerated up to 2 days ahead. If chilled, bake for 30 minutes to reheat.

# DELMONICO POTATOES

*Yield: 8 servings*

*8 medium potatoes*
*Sauce*
*1 cup bread crumbs*
*¼ cup butter, softened*
*Dried parsley flakes*
*1 cup shredded Cheddar cheese*

## Sauce

*6 tablespoons butter or margarine*
*6 tablespoons flour*
*2½ cups half-and-half*
*2 tablespoons dried minced onion*
*1 teaspoon dried parsley*
*¼ teaspoon garlic salt*
*Pepper to taste*
*1 cup shredded Cheddar cheese*

🖝 Peel the potatoes and cut into ⅛- to ¼-inch slices.

🖝 Boil the potatoes in salted water to cover in a saucepan until almost tender; drain.

🖝 For the sauce, melt the butter in a medium saucepan over medium heat. Add the flour. Cook until the flour is dissolved and the sauce is smooth and bubbly, stirring constantly.

🖝 Add the half-and-half gradually, stirring constantly. Increase the heat to medium-high. Cook until thickened, stirring constantly. Add the onion, dried parsley, garlic salt and pepper. Stir in the cheese.

🖝 Combine the potatoes and sauce in a large bowl and mix gently. Pour into a greased 9x13-inch baking dish. Top with the cheese.

🖝 Mix the bread crumbs with the butter in a small bowl. Sprinkle over the potato mixture. Sprinkle with the parsley flakes.

🖝 Bake at 350 degrees for 25 minutes or until bubbly.

## Rebaking Leftover Potatoes

A leftover baked potato can be rebaked if you dip it in water. Bake in a 350-degree oven for about 20 minutes.

## Idaho Potatoes Anna

From *Bound to Please*, Junior League of Boise, 1983

*Yield: 6 to 8 servings*

5 to 6 medium potatoes
2 tablespoons vegetable oil
5 to 6 tablespoons butter
*Beau Monde seasoning to taste*
*Pepper to taste*

### Garnish
*Parsley*

🍃 Peel the potatoes and slice into rounds or ovals; do not cut the potatoes into halves lengthwise before slicing. Slicing may be done by hand or with the medium-thick slicing blade of a food processor.

🍃 Heat the oil and 2 tablespoons of the butter in an au gratin pan or large omelet pan with sloping sides until the butter is melted.

🍃 Place 1 layer of overlapping potato slices in a circular pattern in the prepared pan.

🍃 Sprinkle with seasoning and pepper. Add the remaining potato slices in layers, dotting each layer with the remaining butter and sprinkling with seasoning and pepper.

🍃 Place the pan on the bottom oven rack. Bake at 400 degrees for 15 to 20 minutes. Remove from the oven and cover loosely with foil. Move to the middle oven rack. Bake for 25 to 30 minutes longer or until the potatoes are tender and the mixture is heated through.

🍃 To serve, separate from the edge of the pan and invert onto a large serving platter.

🍃 Garnish with parsley.

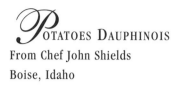

# POTATOES DAUPHINOIS

From Chef John Shields
Boise, Idaho

*Yield: 8 servings*

*3 pounds russet potatoes, peeled,
thinly sliced*
*3 cups whipping cream*
*2 cups milk*
*2 pounds Gruyère cheese,
shredded, divided*
*$1/8$ teaspoon nutmeg, or to taste*
*5 cloves of garlic, crushed*

🌨 Place the potatoes in a greased 3-quart casserole or baking dish with high sides.

🌨 Combine the whipping cream, milk, half the cheese, nutmeg and garlic in a bowl and mix well. Pour over the potatoes. Top with the remaining cheese.

🌨 Cover with foil, being sure that the foil does not touch the cheese.

🌨 Bake at 350 degrees for 50 minutes or until the potatoes are cooked through but not mushy.

🌨 Remove the foil. Bake for 7 to 8 minutes longer or until the top is browned.

## LITERARY TRIVIA

A. A. Milne once said,
"If a fellow really likes
potatoes, he must be
a pretty decent sort
of fellow."

# EGGPLANT AND POTATO BAKE

*Yield: 8 servings as a side dish or*
*4 servings as an entrée*

2 (10 ounces each) eggplant, cut
    into slices
Salt to taste
$^1/_4$ cup olive oil, divided
$^3/_4$ cup finely chopped onion
1 clove of garlic, finely chopped
1 (14-ounce) can chopped tomatoes
1 bunch basil, cut into thin strips
1$^1/_2$ pounds russet potatoes, peeled,
    cut into $^1/_8$-inch slices
7 ounces mozzarella cheese, cut into
    $^1/_8$-inch slices
Freshly ground pepper to taste

☞ Sprinkle the eggplant with salt. Let stand for 30 minutes. Pat dry with paper towels.

☞ Heat 3 tablespoons of the olive oil in a large skillet over medium-high heat. Add the eggplant in batches. Fry until tender and set aside.

☞ Heat the remaining 1 tablespoon olive oil in the skillet. Add the onion and garlic. Sauté briefly. Add the tomatoes. Simmer for 15 minutes. Stir in the basil.

☞ Cook the potatoes in boiling water in a saucepan for 5 minutes. Drain in a colander.

☞ Layer the eggplant, potatoes, cheese and tomato mixture in a greased 2-quart baking dish. Sprinkle with pepper.

☞ Bake at 400 degrees for 40 minutes.

# Au Gratin Potatoes and Peas

*Yield: 6 servings*

*3 cups russet potatoes, peeled, cut*
*into cubes (see Note)*
*¹/₂ to 1 cup bread crumbs*
*1 tablespoon butter or margarine*
*Sauce*
*1 (10-ounce) package frozen peas,*
*thawed, drained*
*1 (2-ounce) jar chopped pimento*

## Sauce

*¹/₄ cup butter or margarine*
*¹/₄ cup flour*
*1 teaspoon salt*
*¹/₈ teaspoon pepper*
*2¹/₄ cups milk*
*4 ounces sharp Cheddar cheese,*
*shredded*

☞ Parboil the potatoes in water to cover in a saucepan; drain and set aside.

☞ Combine the bread crumbs and butter in a small saucepan. Cook until lightly browned. Set aside.

☞ For the sauce, melt the butter in a medium saucepan. Blend in the flour, salt and pepper. Remove from the heat.

☞ Stir in the milk gradually. Cook over medium-high heat until thickened, stirring constantly. Remove from the heat. Add the cheese, stirring until melted.

☞ Combine the potatoes, peas and pimento in a greased 1¹/₂-quart casserole. Pour the sauce over the top. Sprinkle with the bread crumbs.

☞ Bake at 325 degrees for 45 minutes.

☞

*Note: Three cups thawed cube-style frozen processed potatoes may be substituted for the russet potatoes. May add 1¹/₂ cups diced cooked ham to the potato mixture to make a delicious main-dish meal.*

☞

## Scalloped Potatoes

Why do my scalloped potatoes curdle? For one or both of these reasons: 1) The milk or cream was not heated before adding it to the casserole and/or 2) the oven temperature was too high. About 325 to 350 degrees is the correct temperature to forestall curdling.

## Boiling Potatoes

Scrub the potatoes but do not peel them. (Never peel a potato before boiling it; the skin preserves the nutrients and most of the flavor. Let the potato become cool enough to handle and then peel it.) To prevent potatoes from discoloring during boiling, add a touch of lemon juice or salt to the water before cooking.

# DUTCH-OVEN SCALLOPED POTATOES
From Chef Fred Webster, Idaho Rocky Mountain Ranch

*Yield: 8 servings*

*1 cup flour*
*1 quart half-and-half*
*8 medium russet potatoes, cut into $^1/_8$-inch slices*
*1 red onion, cut into $^1/_8$-inch slices*
*Salt and pepper to taste*
*$^1/_2$ cup butter, cut into $^1/_2$-inch cubes*
*8 ounces Cheddar cheese, shredded*

☞ Combine the flour and half-and-half in a bowl and mix well. Pour enough of the mixture into a 12-inch Dutch oven to coat the bottom.

☞ Layer the potatoes, onion, salt, pepper, butter and cheese $^1/_3$ at a time in the Dutch oven.

☞ Pour the remaining half-and-half mixture over the layers.

☞ Cook at camp using charcoal over and under the Dutch oven. May be baked in a conventional oven at 350 degrees for 1 hour.

OLCANNON

A national dish of Ireland

*Yield: 6 servings*

4 medium russet potatoes,
   *peeled, diced*
*3 tablespoons butter or margarine*
*¹/₂ teaspoon salt*
*3 tablespoons milk*
*1 cup water*
*2 cloves of garlic, sliced*
*1¹/₂ cups grated cabbage*
*3 green onions, chopped*

🖝 Cook the potatoes in boiling salted water to cover in a saucepan for 15 to 20 minutes or until tender; drain. Mash the potatoes with the butter, salt and milk.

🖝 Bring 1 cup water to a simmer in a medium saucepan. Add the garlic. Cook for 5 minutes. Add the cabbage and green onions. Cook, covered, for 10 minutes or until the cabbage is tender; drain.

🖝 Combine the cabbage mixture and potatoes in a bowl and mix well.

🖝 Serve immediately or spoon into a buttered 2-quart baking dish and chill for 2 hours or longer to blend the flavors. To reheat, bake at 350 degrees for 25 minutes or until heated through.

## SOFT SKIN

If you enjoy a baked potato with a soft, edible skin, rub vegetable oil on the skin before baking. For a crisply textured potato skin, bake the potato with a clean, dry skin.

## CRISPIER FRIED POTATOES

Prior to frying potatoes, soak them in cold water for 30 minutes or longer. Sprinkle the potatoes lightly with flour and they will fry to a very attractive golden brown.

# POTATOES FLORENTINE

*Yield: 8 servings*

1 (10-ounce) package frozen
   *chopped spinach*
6 medium russet potatoes,
   *cooked, peeled*
*¹/₂ cup butter*
*¹/₂ teaspoon salt*
*¹/₄ teaspoon dill*
*³/₄ cup sour cream*
*¹/₂ cup shredded Cheddar cheese*

🍂 Cook the spinach using the package directions; drain well.

🍂 Mash the potatoes with the butter in a large bowl. Add the spinach, salt, dill and sour cream and mix well.

🍂 Pour into a greased 2-quart baking dish. Sprinkle with the cheese.

🍂 Bake at 325 degrees for 25 minutes.

🍂

*Because this dish has a mild flavor, it would be especially good with seasoned beef tenderloin or a flavorful chicken dish. The leftovers freeze well.*

🍂

# Mashed Potato Soufflé

*Yield: 12 servings*

8 large russet potatoes (about
    4<sup>1</sup>/<sub>2</sub> to 5 pounds)
8 ounces cream cheese, softened
1 cup sour cream
2 teaspoons garlic salt
<sup>1</sup>/<sub>2</sub> teaspoon pepper
<sup>1</sup>/<sub>4</sub> cup butter or margarine
Paprika to taste

🖙 Peel the potatoes and cut into quarters. Combine with 1 inch boiling water in a 5-quart saucepan. Boil until tender; drain. Mash the potatoes in a large bowl.

🖙 Beat the cream cheese and sour cream in a mixer bowl until blended.

🖙 Add the cream cheese mixture, garlic salt and pepper to the potatoes and mix well.

🖙 Spoon into a serving dish or a shallow 3- or 4-quart casserole or baking dish. Dot with the butter. Sprinkle lightly with paprika. (To avoid accidentally using too much paprika, hold the shaker 8 inches above the potatoes.)

🖙 Serve immediately or cover and refrigerate for up to 2 days. To reheat, bring to room temperature. Bake, covered, at 400 degrees for 50 to 60 minutes or until heated through.

🖙 This recipe may be halved and baked in a 2-quart dish. Reheat for 30 minutes.

🖙 This is particularly good served with prime rib.

🖙 For Onion-Flavored Potatoes, add a chopped small onion to the potato mixture; then garnish with French-fried onions.

🖙 For Poppyseed Potatoes, substitute 1 cup shredded Cheddar cheese for the sour cream; add <sup>1</sup>/<sub>4</sub> cup poppy-seeds to the potato mixture with the garlic salt and pepper. Sprinkle with additional poppyseeds and chopped fresh parsley before baking.

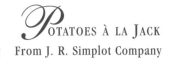

## POTATOES À LA JACK
From J. R. Simplot Company

*Yield: 6 servings*

*2 (4 ounces each) packages*
*    instant potatoes*
*Salt to taste*
*1 (2-ounce) jar pimento*
*¹/₂ cup butter, softened*
*6 ounces cream cheese, softened*
*¹/₄ cup chopped green onions*
*¹/₂ cup grated Parmesan cheese*
*1 green bell pepper, chopped*
*¹/₂ cup shredded Cheddar cheese*
*¹/₄ teaspoon saffron*

🐾 Whip the instant potatoes using the package directions. Season with salt.

🐾 Mince the pimento with its juices.

🐾 Combine the potatoes, pimento, butter, cream cheese, green onions, Parmesan cheese, green pepper, Cheddar cheese and saffron in a bowl and mix well. Spoon into a 1¹/₂-quart casserole.

🐾 Bake at 350 degrees for 30 minutes.

🐾 May be prepared 1 day ahead and stored in the refrigerator until baking time.

 TRIPLE-
CHEESE POTATOES

*Yield: 6 to 8 servings*

*4 medium russet potatoes*
   *(about 1¹/₂ pounds)*
*¹/₄ cup dried bread crumbs*
*1 cup shredded mozzarella cheese*
*1 cup shredded provolone cheese*
*¹/₂ cup hot milk*
*2 tablespoons butter or margarine*
*1 egg yolk*
*¹/₂ teaspoon salt*
*¹/₈ teaspoon pepper*
*1 teaspoon Italian seasoning*
*¹/₂ cup grated Parmesan cheese*

🖎 Peel the potatoes and cut into quarters. Boil or steam until tender; drain.

🖎 Sprinkle the bread crumbs in a greased 5-cup baking dish or round baking pan.

🖎 Mix the mozzarella cheese and provolone cheese in a medium bowl.

🖎 Combine the potatoes, milk, butter, egg yolk, salt, pepper and Italian seasoning in a bowl and mash well.

🖎 Spread half the potato mixture in the prepared baking dish. Sprinkle with half the cheese mixture. Repeat the layers. Top with the Parmesan cheese.

🖎 Bake at 375 degrees for 35 to 40 minutes or until golden brown.

🖎 Serve with any meat main dish.

POTATO TRIVIA

In parts of Ireland, it is traditional to hide a ring in colcannon or boxty. The person who finds the ring is expected to marry within the year.

# BERRY MALLOW YAM BAKE

*Yield: 8 servings*

*1/2 cup flour*
*1/2 cup packed brown sugar*
*1/2 cup rolled oats*
  *(not quick-cooking)*
*1/2 cup chopped pecans*
*1 teaspoon cinnamon*
*1/2 cup butter or margarine, softened*
*2 (29 ounces each) cans yams,*
  *drained*
*2 cups fresh or frozen cranberries*
  *(see Note)*
*1 1/2 cups miniature marshmallows*

🍂 Combine the flour, brown sugar, oats, pecans and cinnamon in a medium bowl. Cut in the butter until crumbly.

🍂 Combine the yams, cranberries and half the brown sugar mixture in a large bowl and mix well.

🍂 Spoon into a greased 2-quart casserole or 9x13-inch baking dish. Top with the remaining brown sugar mixture.

🍂 Bake at 350 degrees for 35 minutes.

🍂 Remove from the oven. Set the oven on Broil.

🍂 Sprinkle the miniature marshmallows over the baked mixture.

🍂 Broil until lightly browned. (Watch carefully to avoid burning the marshmallows.)

🍂

*Note: Drain frozen cranberries well before using.*

🍂

# RALINE SWEET POTATOES

*Yield: 6 to 8 servings*

1 (29-ounce) can sweet potatoes
3 tablespoons butter
$^1/_4$ cup packed brown sugar
$^1/_4$ teaspoon salt
Whipping cream

## Topping

$^2/_3$ cup packed brown sugar
1 tablespoon whipping cream
$^1/_2$ cup chopped pecans
3 tablespoons butter
$^1/_2$ teaspoon ground cinnamon
$^1/_4$ teaspoon ground nutmeg
$^1/_8$ teaspoon salt
$^1/_4$ teaspoon ground ginger
$^1/_8$ teaspoon ground cloves

🖝 Heat the undrained sweet potatoes in a saucepan until heated through; drain.

🖝 Combine with the butter, brown sugar and salt in a bowl. Mash well, adding enough whipping cream to make of the desired consistency.

🖝 Spoon into a buttered 2-quart baking dish.

🖝 For the topping, combine the brown sugar, whipping cream, pecans, butter, cinnamon, nutmeg, salt, ginger and cloves in a small saucepan. Cook over medium heat until the butter is melted, stirring until smooth. Spread over the sweet potatoes.

🖝 Bake at 350 degrees for 10 to 15 minutes or until bubbly.

🖝 An alternative way to prepare this dish is to cut sweet potatoes into $^1/_4$-inch slices and arrange in a buttered baking dish. Spread the topping over the slices and bake for 10 to 15 minutes or until bubbly.

🖝

*Note: This dish can be prepared and refrigerated for up to 2 days before baking. It's great with holiday meals.*

🖝

# Mashed Potato Aioli

A French garlic "mayonnaise"

*Yield: 1½ cups*

*2 large heads of garlic*
*3 quarts water, divided*
*1½ teaspoons salt, divided*
*1 pound russet potatoes, peeled,*
  *cooked, mashed smooth*
*2½ tablespoons olive oil*
*2 to 3 cloves of garlic, or to taste,*
  *peeled, green germ removed*
*Freshly ground pepper to taste*

🐟 Separate and peel the cloves of the garlic heads. Combine with 1 quart of the water in a saucepan. Bring to a boil. Pour off the water and add a second quart to the saucepan. Bring to a boil. Pour off the water and add the third quart of water. Bring to a boil. Add 1 teaspoon of the salt. Reduce the heat. Simmer, covered or uncovered, for 30 to 40 minutes or until the garlic is very tender and the broth is fragrant. Remove from the heat.

🐟 Reserve 2 tablespoons of the garlic broth. Use a slotted spoon to remove the garlic to a food processor fitted with a steel blade. Blend until smooth. Remove to a medium bowl.

🐟 Add the potatoes and mix well. Add the olive oil and reserved broth.

🐟 Place 2 to 3 cloves of garlic and the remaining ½ teaspoon salt in a mortar. Mash into a smooth paste with a pestle. Stir into the potato mixture. Season with additional salt, garlic and pepper.

🐟 This will keep for 3 days in the refrigerator. It is best served fresh as a dip for mounds of small potatoes boiled in their jackets, steamed halibut chunks or shrimp, blanched carrot slices and broccoli florets, chopped celery, halved hard-cooked eggs, and sliced fresh tomatoes. Serve on salad plates with a knife and a fork.

### Garlic Mashed Potatoes

*Yield: 8 servings*

8 medium russet potatoes, peeled,
  cut into pieces
8 cloves of garlic, peeled,
  thinly sliced
5 tablespoons butter or margarine
1 teaspoon salt
Milk
3/4 cup grated Parmesan cheese

#### Garnish
*Sprigs of fresh rosemary*

🖝 Cook the potatoes and garlic in boiling salted water in a saucepan for 20 to 25 minutes or until very tender; drain. Mash with the butter and salt, adding enough milk to make of the desired consistency. Blend in the cheese. Whip with an electric mixer until fluffy.

🖝 Garnish with the rosemary sprigs. Serve immediately.

### Horseradish Mashed Potatoes

*Yield: 8 servings*

8 medium russet potatoes, peeled,
  cut into pieces
5 tablespoons butter or margarine
1 teaspoon salt
Milk
3/4 cup sour cream
3 tablespoons prepared horseradish

🖝 Cook the potatoes in boiling salted water in a saucepan for 20 to 25 minutes or until very tender; drain. Mash with the butter and salt, adding enough milk to make of the desired consistency. Blend in the sour cream and horseradish. Whip with an electric mixer until fluffy.

### Mashed Potatoes and Parsnips

*Yield: 8 servings*

4 medium russet potatoes, peeled,
  cut into pieces
4 parsnips, peeled, cut into pieces
5 tablespoons butter or margarine
1 teaspoon salt
Milk
1 tablespoon bacon bits

🖝 Cook the potatoes and parsnips in boiling salted water in a saucepan for 20 to 25 minutes or until very tender; drain. Mash with the butter and salt, adding enough milk to make of the desired consistency. Mix in the bacon bits. Whip with an electric mixer until fluffy.

## Twice-Baked Russet Potatoes (Basic Recipe)

*Yield: 4 servings*

*4 large russet potatoes*

🐦 Bake the potatoes at 425 degrees for 1 hour. Do not slit, pierce or wrap in foil.

🐦 Remove from the oven. Let cool for 10 minutes or until easily handled.

🐦 Cut a ¹/₂-inch slice lengthwise from the top of each potato and discard.

🐦 Scoop out the potato pulp, leaving a ¹/₂-inch shell intact.

🐦 Mash the pulp with a fork or food processor.

🐦 Combine the potato pulp with the ingredients listed in your chosen variation.

🐦 Spoon the mixture into the shells, piling the mixture ¹/₂ inch above the tops of the skins. At this point, the potatoes may be refrigerated for up to 1 day.

🐦 Place the potatoes on a baking sheet. Bake at 400 degrees for 10 to 15 minutes or until heated through; bake for 25 to 30 minutes if the potatoes were refrigerated.

🐦 Garnish as directed or preferred.

## Broccoli, Buttermilk and Dill Filling

A low-fat option

*2 teaspoons olive oil*
*1¹/₂ cups coarsely chopped*
*   broccoli florets*
*1 cup chopped onion*
*¹/₃ cup low-fat buttermilk*
*¹/₃ cup low-fat sour cream*
*2 tablespoons minced fresh dill, or*
*   2 teaspoons dried*
*1 tablespoon grated*
*   Parmesan cheese*
*¹/₂ teaspoon salt*
*¹/₄ teaspoon pepper*
*¹/₂ cup (2 ounces) shredded*
*   reduced-fat Cheddar cheese*
*Sprigs of fresh dill*

🐦 Prepare the potatoes as directed in the Basic Recipe.

🐦 Heat the olive oil in a medium nonstick skillet over medium heat. Add the broccoli and onion. Sauté for 4 minutes or until tender.

🐦 Fill the potato shells with a mixture of the potato pulp, broccoli, onion, buttermilk, sour cream, dill, Parmesan cheese, salt, pepper and Cheddar cheese. Reheat as directed in the Basic Recipe. Top with fresh dill sprigs.

## Cheddar Onion Filling

*1 cup shredded Cheddar cheese*
*¹/₂ cup low-fat cottage cheese or*
*   light sour cream*
*¹/₄ cup margarine, softened*
*2 tablespoons chopped green onions*
*Paprika to taste*

🐦 Prepare the potatoes as directed in the Basic Recipe. Fill the shells with a mixture of the potato pulp, Cheddar cheese, cottage cheese, margarine and green onions. Sprinkle with paprika before reheating. Reheat as directed in the Basic Recipe.

## Cheese and Corn Filling

2 teaspoons olive oil

1 cup chopped leeks

1 cup chopped onion

2 cloves of garlic, minced

³/₄ cup frozen whole kernel corn,
    thawed, drained

¹/₂ cup 1% low-fat cottage cheese

¹/₂ cup plain fat-free yogurt

¹/₂ teaspoon salt

¹/₄ teaspoon ground red pepper

🍂 Prepare the potatoes as directed in the Basic Recipe.

🍂 Heat the olive oil in a medium nonstick skillet over medium-high heat. Add the leeks, onion and garlic. Sauté for 4 minutes or until tender.

🍂 Fill the potato shells with a mixture of the potato pulp, leek mixture, corn, cottage cheese, yogurt, salt and pepper. Reheat as directed in the Basic Recipe.

## Vegetable Filling

1 tablespoon margarine

1 cup julienned carrot

1 cup thinly sliced green or
    red bell pepper

¹/₄ teaspoon Italian seasoning

1 cup julienned zucchini

2 ounces low-fat Monterey Jack
    cheese, shredded

🍂 Prepare the potatoes as directed in the Basic Recipe.

🍂 Heat the margarine in a medium skillet over medium-high heat. Add the carrot, bell pepper and Italian seasoning. Sauté until the vegetables are tender-crisp.

🍂 Add the zucchini. Sauté for 1 minute or until the zucchini is tender.

🍂 Fill the potato shells with a mixture of the potato pulp and zucchini mixture. Reheat as directed in the Basic Recipe. Top with the cheese.

## Mexican-Style Filling

1 (4-ounce) can chopped green
    chiles, drained

3 hard-cooked eggs, chopped

¹/₂ cup butter, softened

1 cup sour cream

¹/₂ cup shredded Longhorn cheese

🍂 Prepare the potatoes as directed in the Basic Recipe. Fill the shells with a mixture of the potato pulp, green chiles, eggs, butter and sour cream. Top with the cheese. Reheat as directed in the Basic Recipe.

### Bleu Cheese and Bacon Filling

*1/2 cup sour cream*
*1/4 cup crumbled bleu cheese*
*1/4 cup milk*
*1/4 cup butter, softened*
*3/4 teaspoon salt*
*1/8 teaspoon pepper, or to taste*
*4 slices bacon, crisp-fried, crumbled*

☞ Prepare the potatoes as directed in the Basic Recipe. Fill the shells with a mixture of the potato pulp, sour cream, cheese, milk, butter, salt and pepper. Reheat as directed in the Basic Recipe.

☞ Top with the bacon.

### Brie Filling

*2 1/2 ounces Brie cheese, cut into*
   *1-inch cubes*
*1/4 cup butter, softened*
*1 egg yolk*
*2 tablespoons minced green onion*
   *tops, divided*
*1/2 teaspoon salt*
*1/4 teaspoon pepper*
*1/4 teaspoon nutmeg*

☞ Prepare the potatoes as directed in the Basic Recipe. Fill the shells with a mixture of the potato pulp, cheese, butter, egg yolk, half the green onions, salt, pepper and nutmeg. Reheat as directed in the Basic Recipe.

☞ Sprinkle with the remaining green onions. Broil 5 inches from the heat source for 3 to 5 minutes or until puffy and lightly browned.

### Fat-Free Jalapeño Filling

*2 fresh jalapeño peppers,*
   *seeded, minced*
*3 carrots, cooked, mashed*
   *(about 3/4 cup)*
*1 cup fat-free sour cream*
*1/4 cup chopped green onion tops*
*3/8 teaspoon Tabasco sauce, or*
   *to taste*
*1 teaspoon salt*
*1/2 teaspoon black pepper*
*1/8 teaspoon cayenne, or to taste*

☞ Prepare the potatoes as directed in the Basic Recipe. Fill the shells with a mixture of the potato pulp, jalapeños, carrots, sour cream, green onions, Tabasco sauce, salt, black pepper and cayenne. Reheat as directed in the Basic Recipe.

# ROASTED POTATOES (BASIC RECIPE)

*Yield: 4 servings*

*4 medium russet potatoes or other
    potatoes of your choice*
*2 tablespoons olive oil*
*$^1/_2$ teaspoon salt, flavored salt or salt
    seasoning*
*$^1/_8$ teaspoon pepper*

☞ Wash the potatoes and cut into $^3/_4$-inch pieces. Pat dry. The potatoes may be used peeled or unpeeled.

☞ Mix the potatoes, olive oil, salt and pepper in a bowl.

☞ Arrange the potatoes in a single layer in a shallow 10x15-inch baking pan.

☞ Roast at 450 degrees for 45 to 60 minutes or until tender and browned, stirring every 15 to 20 minutes.

## Roasted Potatoes and Red Bell Pepper with Sage and Garlic

*Basic Recipe ingredients*
*4 teaspoons minced fresh sage*
*2 to 4 large cloves of garlic, minced*
*$^1/_4$ cup red bell pepper, cut into
    $^1/_2$-inch pieces*
*2 tablespoons grated
    Parmesan cheese*
*Sprigs of fresh parsley*

☞ Mix the potatoes, olive oil, salt, pepper, sage and garlic in a bowl.

☞ Roast as directed in the Basic Recipe for 25 minutes. Add the red pepper and toss gently. Roast for 20 to 35 minutes longer.

☞ Top with the cheese and parsley.

## Rosemary- and Garlic-Roasted Potatoes

*Basic Recipe ingredients*
*1 tablespoon snipped fresh
    rosemary, or 1$^1/_2$ teaspoons
    crushed dried rosemary*
*2 cloves of garlic, minced*

☞ Mix the potatoes, olive oil, salt, pepper, rosemary and garlic in a bowl.

☞ Roast as directed in the Basic Recipe.

## Roasted Potatoes with Marinated Artichokes and Garlic

*2 (6 ounces each) jars marinated artichoke hearts*
*Basic Recipe ingredients (see Note)*
*1 head of garlic, separated into cloves, peeled*
*1 tablespoon gently crushed fresh rosemary, or 1/2 teaspoon dried*

☞ Drain the artichoke hearts, reserving 1/4 cup marinade. Cut the larger artichoke hearts into halves.
☞ Mix the potatoes, salt, pepper, reserved marinade, artichoke hearts, garlic and rosemary in a bowl.
☞ Roast, covered, at 450 degrees for 15 minutes. Roast, uncovered, for 35 to 50 minutes or until tender and browned.

☞

*Note: Omit the olive oil in this variation.*

☞

## Onion-Roasted Thyme Potatoes

*Basic Recipe ingredients*
*1 large yellow, white or red onion, peeled, cut into 3/4-inch chunks, or 1 cup pearl onions, peeled or left whole*
*1 1/2 teaspoons fresh thyme leaves, or 1 teaspoon dried (see Note)*

☞ Mix the potatoes, olive oil, salt, pepper, onion and thyme in a bowl.
☞ Roast as directed in the Basic Recipe.
☞ Serve with catsup or a mixture of nonfat yogurt and barbecue sauce.

☞

*Note: If you grow lemon thyme in your herb garden, try using it in this recipe for a different taste.*

☞

## Garlic-Roasted Potatoes and Greens

*3 to 4 cups watercress sprigs, rinsed*
*Basic Recipe ingredients*
*2 tablespoons olive oil*
*4 large cloves of garlic, peeled, cut into quarters lengthwise*
*3 tablespoons wine vinegar*
*2 tablespoons chopped chives or green onion tops*

☞ Chop half the watercress; set aside.
☞ Mix the potatoes, all the olive oil, salt, pepper and garlic in a bowl.
☞ Roast as directed in the Basic Recipe. Remove from the oven.
☞ Pour the vinegar into the pan. Scrape with a spatula to release the browned bits; mix with the potatoes. Stir the chopped watercress into the potatoes. Arrange the remaining watercress around the potatoes. Sprinkle with the chives.
☞ Serve slightly warm to hot.

## Lemon-Roasted Potatoes

*Basic Recipe ingredients*
*1 lemon, very thinly sliced*
*2 sprigs (or more) of fresh rosemary,*
*    crushed, or 1 teaspoon*
*    (or more) dried*
*1 clove (or more) of garlic, minced*

☞ Mix the potatoes, olive oil, salt, pepper, lemon, rosemary and garlic in a bowl.
☞ Roast as directed in the Basic Recipe.

## Anchovy-Roasted Potatoes

*Basic Recipe ingredients*
*2 tablespoons chopped fresh thyme,*
*    or 2 teaspoons dried*
*4 teaspoons anchovy paste*
*1 clove of garlic, minced*

☞ Mix the potatoes, olive oil, salt, pepper, thyme, anchovy paste and garlic in a bowl.
☞ Arrange the potatoes on a baking sheet so that they are not touching. Roast as directed in the Basic Recipe.

## Coriander-Roasted Potatoes

*Basic Recipe ingredients*
*2 teaspoons ground dried coriander*
*1/4 cup chopped fresh cilantro*

☞ Mix the potatoes, olive oil, salt and pepper in a bowl. Roast as directed in the Basic Recipe.
☞ Stir in the coriander and cilantro.

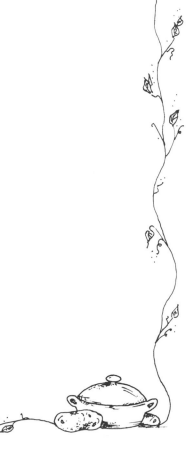

## Red-Hot Parmesan Potatoes

*Basic Recipe ingredients*
*1 teaspoon crushed dried red pepper*
*1/2 cup freshly grated*
*    Parmesan cheese*
*1/4 cup chopped fresh basil*

☞ Mix the potatoes, olive oil, salt, black pepper and red pepper in a bowl.
☞ Roast as directed in the Basic Recipe.
☞ Sprinkle with the cheese and basil.

## Roasted Potatoes Dijon

*Basic Recipe ingredients*
*2 cloves of garlic, coarsely chopped*
*2 tablespoons melted butter or*
    *margarine*
*$^1$/$_3$ cup Dijon mustard or*
    *country-style Dijon mustard*
*$^1$/$_4$ cup chopped parsley*

🖎 Mix the potatoes, olive oil, salt, pepper, garlic, butter and Dijon mustard in a bowl.

🖎 Roast as directed in the Basic Recipe.

🖎 Sprinkle with the parsley.

🖎 Serve immediately.

## ROASTED SWEET AND WHITE POTATOES

*Yield: 12 servings*

*1 pound russet potatoes, peeled, cut*
    *into 1-inch chunks*
*1 pound sweet potatoes or yams,*
    *peeled, cut into 1-inch chunks*
*$^1$/$_4$ cup melted butter*
*$^1$/$_4$ cup olive oil*
*1 large onion, peeled,*
    *cut into eighths*
*8 cloves of garlic, peeled,*
    *cut into halves*
*$^1$/$_2$ cup coarsely chopped hazelnuts*
    *(see Note)*
*Salt to taste*

🖎 Mix the potatoes, sweet potatoes, butter, olive oil, onion and garlic in a large bowl. Spread in a 10x15-inch baking dish or shallow roasting pan.

🖎 Bake on the bottom oven rack at 475 degrees for 30 minutes, stirring twice. At this point, may be left standing for up to 4 hours.

🖎 Stir in the hazelnuts. Bake for 15 to 20 minutes longer, stirring twice. The potatoes should be tender and very slightly browned.

🖎 Season with salt.

🖎 This recipe may be divided to make 6 servings.

🖎

*Note: Walnuts or pecans may be used in this recipe, but hazelnuts are preferred.*

🖎

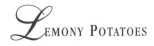 ## LEMONY POTATOES

*Yield: 4 to 6 servings*

2 pounds russet potatoes, cut into
    2-inch pieces (see Note)
1/4 cup olive oil
2 tablespoons fresh lemon juice
Grated peel of 1/2 lemon
Salt and pepper to taste
1 teaspoon dried oregano

### Garnish
Chopped parsley or dill

🖋 Cook the potatoes in boiling water to cover in a saucepan just until tender. Drain and return to the saucepan.

🖋 Shake the saucepan over medium heat until the potatoes are dry. Remove to a heated serving dish to keep warm.

🖋 Combine the olive oil, lemon juice, lemon peel, salt, pepper and oregano in a bowl. Pour over the potatoes, stirring to coat well.

🖋 Garnish with the parsley.

🖋 Serve warm, at room temperature or chilled.

🖋 Serve this very versatile dish with fish or chicken.

🖋

*Note: The potatoes may be peeled or unpeeled.*

🖋

## POTATO TRIVIA

On average, it takes

120 days to grow an

Idaho potato.

## POTATOES IN PARSLEY SAUCE
A Basque favorite

*Yield: 4 servings*

*¹/₂ cup finely chopped onion*
*2 cloves of garlic, pressed*
*2 tablespoons vegetable oil*
*4 medium potatoes, cut into*
  *¹/₄-inch slices*
*¹/₄ cup minced parsley*
*²/₃ cup chicken stock or broth*
*1 teaspoon salt*
*¹/₄ teaspoon pepper*
*2 hard-cooked eggs, chopped*

🖝 Cook the onion and garlic in the oil in a large saucepan until the onion is golden brown, stirring occasionally.

🖝 Add the potatoes and parsley. Cook for 5 to 7 minutes, stirring constantly but gently.

🖝 Add the chicken stock, salt and pepper. Bring to a boil; reduce the heat. Simmer, covered, for 15 minutes or until the potatoes are tender.

🖝 Sprinkle with the eggs.

🖝

*These potatoes were served at The Delamar, a well-known Basque boarding house that stood at 807 Grove Street in one of downtown Boise's most fashionable neighborhoods. Among the owners of this house were C. W. Moore, its builder and the founder of the Idaho First National Bank; Joseph R. Delamar, celebrated mining capitalist; W. E. Pierce, developer and mayor; William E. Borah, Idaho senator; and Mateo and Adriana Arregui, Basque proprietors of the house for many years.*

🖝

## ARAMELIZED POTATOES

*Yield: 8 servings*

*16 small new potatoes*
*1/2 cup packed brown sugar*
*1/3 cup melted butter*
*1/2 teaspoon salt*
*Minced fresh dill to taste*

🍂 Boil or steam the potatoes until tender. Let cool and peel.

🍂 Combine the brown sugar, butter and salt in a large skillet. Cook over medium heat for 5 minutes or until thickened, stirring constantly.

🍂 Add the potatoes. Reduce the heat to low. Shake the skillet frequently until the potatoes are thoroughly coated.

🍂 Place the potatoes in a heated bowl. Sprinkle with dill.

## NEW POTATOES AND PEAS

*Yield: 4 servings*

*10 small new red or white potatoes, peeled*
*2 cups fresh or frozen peas*
*1/2 teaspoon salt*
*1/4 teaspoon pepper*
*1 tablespoon flour*
*1 teaspoon water*
*1/4 cup whipping cream*
*1 tablespoon butter or margarine*

🍂 Parboil the potatoes in water to cover in a saucepan. Add the peas. Cook for 10 to 15 minutes or until the potatoes are tender; drain. Return the potatoes and peas to the saucepan. Add the salt and pepper.

🍂 Mix the flour and water into a thin paste in a small bowl. Stir into the potatoes and peas. Cook over medium-low heat for 3 to 4 minutes or until heated through, stirring constantly.

🍂 Add the whipping cream and butter. Cook until heated through.

*(continued on next page)*

# POTATO RISSOLES

*Yield: 8 servings*

2 cups finely chopped onions
2 cloves of garlic, minced
¼ cup plus 2 tablespoons vegetable oil, divided
2 cups mashed cooked potatoes
2 cups finely ground hazelnuts
2 tablespoons chopped fresh basil
1½ cups cornmeal

🍳 Cook the onions and garlic in 2 tablespoons of the oil in a medium skillet until tender. Let cool.
🍳 Mix the potatoes with the hazelnuts in a medium bowl. Add the onion mixture and basil and mix well.
🍳 Shape the mixture into balls. Roll in the cornmeal.
🍳 Fry in the remaining ¼ cup oil in the skillet, adding additional oil if needed.
🍳 Serve on the side with a salad.

# CALCUTTA POTATOES

*Yield: 6 servings*

5 large russet potatoes, peeled, cut into ½-inch chunks
2 teaspoons mustard seeds
2 tablespoons butter
2 teaspoons ground cumin
Salt and pepper to taste
1 jalapeño, seeded, sliced
1 teaspoon grated fresh ginger
½ lime

🍳 Combine the potatoes, mustard seeds and butter in a skillet. Cook until the potatoes are almost tender and the mixture is browned. Add the cumin. Cook for 5 minutes. Season with salt and pepper.
🍳 Toss the hot potatoes with the jalapeño and ginger in a bowl. Squeeze the lime over the mixture.
🍳 These flavors are fresh and fiery. This dish is also excellent reheated the next day.

# LATKES

*Yield: 6 servings*

6 cups grated russet potatoes
   (see Note)
2 cups chopped onions (see Note)
1¹/₂ cups flour
Salt and pepper to taste
3 large eggs, slightly beaten
Vegetable oil for frying

🍂 Rinse and dry the potatoes.

🍂 Combine the potatoes, onions, flour, salt, pepper and eggs in a bowl and mix well, adding additional flour if the mixture is too soft.

🍂 Heat the oil to medium-hot in a large skillet. Drop the potato mixture by large spoonfuls into the oil. Cook until browned on both sides. Blot with paper towels.

🍂 Serve hot with applesauce and sour cream.

🍂

*Note: Try frozen processed hash browns and frozen chopped onions in this recipe.*

🍂

continuous use. In 1986, Congregation Beth Israel and Congregation Ahavath Israel merged to form Ahavath Beth Israel, the center of Judaism in Idaho. Incidentally, the first Jewish governor in the USA was Idaho's Moses Alexander, 1915–1919.

# Desserts

## Julia Child, My Mother Wasn't

My mom always told me that good home cooking was the secret to a great marriage, which probably explains why my new step-father orders Chinese take-out so often. Mom, bless her little heart, was, to be politically correct, culinarially challenged.

While I was young I couldn't tell the difference between a radish and a beet, but potatoes were well known to me. My mom's idea of a variety of vegetables was potatoes — mashed, baked, hashed, boiled, French-fried and burned. Even though I earned a master's degree in potatoes by surviving my mom's potato cooking, I was not familiar with, nor prepared for, Mom's crowning achievement: the Ever Tasty Potato Cookie Pastry.

I am sure there are talented people out there who can easily make the potato into a dessert; my mother was not one of them. While I can't recall exactly what the potato cookie concoction was (the years have erased that and several other curious Mom facts from my brain), I distinctly recall the reaction of others upon sampling it. My family would take a single bite of the cookie, wait until the cramps in their eyebrows and cheeks subsided, and then excitedly declare, "Boy am I stuffed!"

Undeterred by our lack of wholehearted endorsement, Mom would decorate the cookie pastries with green and red sugar sprinkles and set off for the annual Christmas cookie exchange.

The holiday cookie exchange was a long and distinguished tradition in our neighborhood. The ritual required each participant to provide a cookie, or other dessert item, to exchange with each of the other participants. Upon arrival, everyone would display their proud creations on a large table.

For my mother, the annual exchange presented a significant challenge, simultaneously tapping her creativity and her ability to bake. Eventually, after many less than successful contributions to the cookie exchange, evolved what I call "Mom's Handy Tips for Holiday Food Exchanges," aka "Holiday Tips for the Culinarially Challenged Kitchen Engineer." They are:

1) Never use an identifiable family plate. Buy one, use plastic, whatever, but be fully prepared to abandon the plate.

2) Even if they ask you to tape your name to the bottom of your plate, don't. Reason? See rule #1.

3) Always cover your dessert with tin foil. Plastic wrap is transparent and allows too much time for identification of your dessert while you are still holding it. Tin foil will protect the anonymity of your dessert as long as possible.

4) Go heavy on the sugar sprinkles. Aside from the obvious aesthetic value, sugar sprinkles are wonderful for covering up, or I mean, enhancing the natural taste of your dessert.

5) Always bring fewer dessert items than requested. This way it immediately looks as if some of your desserts have already been taken, thereby creating the impression someone has actually eaten them. The added bonus here is that it will reduce the likelihood of people commenting on your dessert, not knowing who among them has tasted it.

6) Always set your dessert display near the table's edge. If experience taught Mom anything, it was that it's much easier to slyly remove untouched desserts (or an entire plate) off the edge of the table than from the center.

7) As the party winds down, initiate the cleanup voluntarily. Not only will this create the impression you are downright thoughtful, it will provide

you with an excellent opportunity to quietly discard your untouched desserts without anyone noticing.

8) Finally, if anyone is becoming suspicious of your culinary talents, then it is probably time to visit a bakery near you.

Well, that's it, the tips are probably the most significant contribution Mom ever made to the cookie exchange tradition. Utilizing these simple tips, Mom has managed to elude holiday embarrassment year in and year out. To this day she continues to receive her invitation to the annual cookie exchange, although they did give up asking her to bring her "cookies" years ago.

— *by Derrick O'Neill*

## APRICOT-FILLED CHOCOLATE POTATO CAKE

*Yield: 16 servings*

### Cake
*1 (2-layer) package devil's food cake mix (see Note)*
*³/₄ cup dry mashed potato flakes*
*2 cups water*
*2 eggs*

### Filling
*¹/₄ cup apricot preserves*

### Chocolate Glaze
*1 cup confectioners' sugar*
*¹/₄ cup chocolate syrup*
*1 teaspoon vanilla extract*

🍮 For the cake, combine the cake mix, potato flakes, water and eggs in a large mixer bowl. Beat at low speed just until moistened. Beat at high speed for 2 minutes.

🍮 Pour the batter into 2 greased and floured 9-inch round cake pans.

🍮 Bake at 350 degrees for 25 to 30 minutes or until a wooden pick inserted near the center comes out clean. Cool slightly. Remove from the pans to cool completely.

🍮 For the filling, melt the preserves in a saucepan over low heat.

🍮 Place 1 cake layer on a serving platter. Spread with the preserves. Top with the remaining layer.

🍮 For the glaze, combine the confectioners' sugar, chocolate syrup and vanilla in a small bowl, stirring until smooth. Spoon over the cake, allowing some of the glaze to run down the side of the cake.

🍮

*Note: This cake is also good prepared with low-fat devil's food cake mix. Instead of the Chocolate Glaze, try fat-free fudge topping.*

🍮

## CHOCOLATE SPICE POTATO CAKE

*Yield: 12 servings*

### Cake

*2 cups flour*
*2 teaspoons baking powder*
*1 teaspoon nutmeg*
*1 teaspoon cinnamon*
*1/2 teaspoon salt*
*2 cups sugar*
*2/3 cup shortening*
*3 eggs*
*1 cup mashed cooked potatoes,*
*    cooled*
*1/2 cup baking cocoa*
*1/2 cup milk*
*1 cup chopped walnuts*

### Frosting

*3 ounces unsweetened chocolate*
*3 tablespoons butter*
*1/4 cup hot water, cream or coffee*
*1/8 teaspoon salt*
*2 cups confectioners' sugar*
*1 teaspoon vanilla extract*

🍃 For the cake, mix the flour, baking powder, nutmeg, cinnamon and salt together.

🍃 Cream the sugar, shortening and eggs in a mixer bowl until light and fluffy. Add the potatoes, cocoa and milk and mix well.

🍃 Add the flour mixture gradually to the creamed mixture, mixing well after each addition. Fold in the walnuts. Pour into a greased 9x13-inch cake pan.

🍃 Bake at 350 degrees for 25 to 35 minutes or until a wooden pick inserted near the center comes out clean. Let cool.

🍃 For the frosting, melt the chocolate in a saucepan over very low heat. Add the butter. Cook until the butter is melted. Remove from the heat.

🍃 Stir in the hot water and salt. Add the confectioners' sugar and vanilla gradually, mixing well after each addition until of a spreading consistency.

🍃 Spread over the cooled cake.

# Potato Mocha Pound Cake

*Yield: 16 servings*

1 tablespoon instant coffee powder
2 tablespoons hot water
1¹/₂ cups low-fat milk
2 cups flour
2 cups sugar
1 cup instant potato flakes
4 teaspoons baking powder
¹/₂ teaspoon salt
1 (4-ounce) package chocolate
   instant pudding mix
1 cup butter, softened
4 eggs

☞ Combine the coffee powder and hot water in a cup, stirring until the coffee powder is dissolved. Mix with the milk in a small bowl.

☞ Combine the flour, sugar, potato flakes, baking powder, salt, pudding mix, butter and eggs in a large mixer bowl. Beat at low speed until mixed. Beat in the milk mixture. Beat at medium speed for 4 minutes. Pour into a greased and floured 10-inch bundt pan.

☞ Bake at 350 degrees for 50 to 55 minutes or until a wooden pick inserted near the center comes out clean.

☞ Cool in the pan for 30 minutes. Invert onto a serving platter.

☞ Top with ice cream with Kahlúa or with a chocolate glaze.

☞

*Note: Be sure to grease and flour the bundt pan, even if it has a nonstick lining.*

☞

## SPACE

During a sixteen-day mission in October 1995, NASA's Columbia shuttle crew grew edible potato tubers in a controlled space atmosphere. This means that potatoes were the first food to be grown in space! It is now feasible that potato plants will provide the oxygen necessary for astronauts' life support on future long term missions.

## Sweet Potato Pie with Bourbon Sauce

*Yield: 8 servings*

### Pie

1/4 cup bourbon
1 cup plus 1 tablespoon (about)
    evaporated milk
2 eggs
1 1/2 cups mashed cooked sweet
    potatoes
3/4 cup sugar
1/2 teaspoon salt
1 teaspoon ground cinnamon
1/2 teaspoon ground nutmeg
1/2 teaspoon ground ginger
1/4 teaspoon ground cloves
1 unbaked (9-inch) pie shell

### Bourbon Sauce

1 1/2 cups whipping cream
1 cup milk
1 (4-ounce) package vanilla instant
    pudding mix
3 tablespoons bourbon, brandy
    or rum
1 teaspoon vanilla extract

☞ For the pie, mix the bourbon with enough evaporated milk to measure 1 1/3 cups.

☞ Combine the eggs, sweet potatoes, sugar, salt, cinnamon, nutmeg, ginger, cloves and bourbon mixture in a large bowl in the order given and mix well. Pour into the pie shell.

☞ Bake at 450 degrees for 15 minutes. Reduce the oven temperature to 350 degrees. Bake for 45 minutes or until the center of the filling is set.

☞ Let cool. Chill until serving time.

☞ For the sauce, combine the whipping cream and milk in a large bowl. Whip in the pudding mix gradually.

☞ Add the bourbon and vanilla and whip until the mixture is the consistency of a sauce (not as firm as pudding, but not runny).

☞ Let stand for 1 hour to thicken.

☞ Serve the sauce with the pie.

☞

*Note: This delicious sauce would be good on other desserts, too.*

☞

 # Yam Pecan Pie

*Yield: 6 to 8 servings*

## Topping

*¹/₄ cup butter, softened*
*¹/₂ cup packed brown sugar*
*³/₄ cup finely chopped pecans*

## Pie

*1 cup mashed cooked or canned*
*    sweet potatoes (see Note)*
*¹/₃ cup packed brown sugar*
*³/₄ teaspoon cinnamon*
*¹/₈ teaspoon salt*
*1 (5-ounce) can evaporated milk*
*2 eggs, beaten*
*1 unbaked (9-inch) pie shell*
*Whipped cream (optional)*

☞ For the topping, mix the butter, brown sugar and pecans in a bowl until crumbly. Set aside.

☞ For the pie filling, combine the sweet potatoes, brown sugar, cinnamon, salt, evaporated milk and eggs in a large bowl and mix well. Pour into the pie shell.

☞ Bake at 375 degrees for 20 minutes. Sprinkle with the topping. Bake for 25 minutes longer.

☞ Let cool. Serve with whipped cream.

☞

*Note: If using fresh sweet potatoes, add ¹/₃ cup sugar to the sweet potatoes. Cool slightly before mixing with the other ingredients.*

☞

## COOKING TIP

Immediately after peeling sweet potatoes, place them in salted water to keep them from turning dark.

# OATMEAL POTATO CINNAMON DROPS

*Yield: 5 dozen*

*2 cups flour*
*2 teaspoons cinnamon*
*$^1/_2$ teaspoon baking soda*
*1 cup butter, softened*
*2 cups sugar*
*2 eggs*
*1 tablespoon molasses*
*2 teaspoons vanilla extract*
*1$^1/_2$ cups quick-cooking oats*
*1 cup instant potato flakes*
*1 cup chopped walnuts*
*$^2/_3$ cup raisins or dates*
*$^1/_2$ cup semisweet chocolate chips*

🍂 Sift the flour, cinnamon and baking soda together.

🍂 Cream the butter and sugar in a mixer bowl until light and fluffy. Beat in the eggs. Add the molasses and vanilla, stirring until mixed.

🍂 Add the flour mixture to the creamed mixture gradually, beating well after each addition.

🍂 Stir in the oats, potato flakes, walnuts, raisins and chocolate chips and mix well; this mixture will be stiff.

🍂 Drop by heaping tablespoons 2 inches apart on a nonstick cookie sheet.

🍂 Bake at 350 degrees for 12 minutes.

# Potato Chocolate Cherry Bars

*Yield: 24 bars*

1 (2-layer) package chocolate
    cake mix
1 cup Ore-Ida frozen mashed
    potatoes (do not add milk)
1 (21-ounce) can cherry pie filling
1 teaspoon almond extract

## Frosting
1 cup sugar
2 tablespoons butter or margarine
3 tablespoons (or more) milk
$^1/_3$ cup semisweet chocolate chips

🖙 Prepare the cake mix using the package directions and decreasing the water to 1 cup.

🖙 Add the potatoes, pie filling and flavoring and mix well.

🖙 Pour into a 9x13-inch baking pan sprayed with nonstick cooking spray.

🖙 Bake at 350 degrees for 30 to 35 minutes or until the dessert tests done.

🖙 For the frosting, combine the sugar, butter and milk in a small saucepan. Boil for 1 minute, stirring occasionally. Remove from the heat.

🖙 Add the chocolate chips, stirring until smooth.

🖙 Pour over the warm dessert. Cut into bars.

🖙

*Note: May omit the frosting and sprinkle with confectioners' sugar when cool. May be served as a cake, with a yield of 15 servings.*

🖙

# Potato Oat Bars

*Yield: 12 servings*

1 cup quick-cooking oats
3/4 cup flour
1/4 teaspoon salt
1/4 teaspoon baking soda
1/2 cup butter, softened
1/2 cup packed brown sugar
1/2 teaspoon vanilla extract
1 egg, slightly beaten
3/4 cup mashed cooked sweet potato
1/4 cup mashed cooked russet potato
2/3 cup sweetened condensed milk
1 teaspoon pumpkin pie spice
1/2 teaspoon grated orange peel
1/4 cup chopped walnuts

🐟 Mix the oats, flour, salt and baking soda together.

🐟 Cream the butter, brown sugar and vanilla in a mixer bowl until light and fluffy.

🐟 Add the flour mixture to the creamed mixture, stirring until crumbly. Pat 1 1/2 cups over the bottom of a greased 9x9-inch baking pan.

🐟 Bake at 350 degrees for 10 minutes.

🐟 Combine the egg, sweet potato, potato, condensed milk, pumpkin pie spice and orange peel in a medium bowl and mix well. Pour over the baked layer.

🐟 Mix the walnuts with the remaining crumb mixture. Sprinkle over the top of the dessert.

🐟 Bake for 25 to 30 minutes longer or until golden brown.

🐟 Let cool. Cut into bars.

#  POTATO CHIP COOKIES

*Yield: 4 dozen*

2 cups firmly packed brown sugar,
    or 1 cup packed brown sugar and
    1 cup sugar
1 cup butter, softened
2 eggs
2 cups flour
1 teaspoon baking soda
1 teaspoon vanilla extract
1 cup crushed potato chips
1 cup chopped nuts (optional)
1 cup semisweet chocolate chips or
    milk chocolate chips

☞ Cream the brown sugar, butter and eggs in a mixer bowl until light and fluffy.

☞ Stir in the flour, baking soda and vanilla and mix well.

☞ Add the potato chips, nuts and chocolate chips and mix well.

☞ Drop by teaspoonfuls onto nonstick cookie sheets.

☞ Bake at 350 degrees for 10 to 12 minutes or until browned.

☞

*Note: At last! A tasty way to use up the potato chips left in the bottom of the bag.*

☞

## THE FIRST POTATO CHIP

The first potato chip was created in the nineteenth century after a New York chef was insulted by a patron who disliked a dish of fried potatoes. The patron complained that the fried potatoes were too thick. The chef, in spite, went back and made the first thinly sliced potato, now known as our potato chip.

## SPUDS

No one knows for sure where "spuds," the slang name for potatoes, comes from. One possible answer is that the barrel of potatoes at the end of a processing line was labeled SPUDS, an acronym for Some Potatoes Under Desirable Standards. Or, possibly, the acronym could have come from the Society for Prevention of Unwholesome Diets, so named to prevent another Irish famine.

# SPUDNUTS

*Yield: 2 dozen doughnuts*

## Doughnuts
*4¹/₂ teaspoons dry yeast*
*1 cup lukewarm water*
*²/₃ cup melted butter or margarine,*
  *cooled*
*¹/₂ cup sugar*
*1 teaspoon salt*
*1 cup mashed cooked potatoes*
*2 eggs*
*1 cup scalded milk, cooled*
*5 to 6 cups flour*
*Vegetable oil for deep-frying*

## Glaze
*2 (16 ounces each) packages*
  *confectioners' sugar*
*¹/₈ teaspoon salt*
*1 cup hot milk*
*2 teaspoons vanilla extract*

☞ For the doughnuts, dissolve the yeast in the lukewarm water. Combine with the butter, sugar, salt, potatoes, eggs, milk and flour and mix until a soft dough forms. Let rise.

☞ Knead the dough down. Let rise until doubled in bulk.

☞ Roll ¹/₂ inch thick on a lightly floured surface. Cut into desired shape.

☞ Let rise for 30 minutes.

☞ Deep-fry in the oil in a deep fryer or skillet until golden brown. Drain and let cool.

☞ For the glaze, combine the confectioners' sugar, salt, milk and vanilla in a bowl and mix until of the desired consistency.

☞ Drizzle the glaze over the cooled spudnuts.

# Potato Blintzes

*Yield: 16 blintzes*

## Blintzes

*1/3 pound russet potatoes, peeled, cut*
  *into 1-inch cubes (about 1 cup)*
*3 eggs*
*1/2 teaspoon salt*
*3/4 cup flour*
*1 1/2 cups water*
*1 tablespoon vanilla extract*
*Vegetable oil*

## Filling

*3/4 cup cottage cheese*
*1/2 cup sugar*
*1 1/2 tablespoons grated orange peel*
*Fruit topping or canned pie filling*

🖎 For the blintzes, cook the potatoes in water to cover in a saucepan for 15 minutes or until tender; drain.

🖎 Mash the potatoes until very smooth. Add the eggs and salt. Add the flour and water alternately, mixing well after each addition. Add the vanilla. Let stand, covered, for 1 hour.

🖎 Grease a large skillet with oil. Heat over medium-high heat. Pour 3 tablespoons of the batter into the hot skillet. Tilt the skillet quickly to spread the batter evenly. Cook for 1 minute or until the bottom of the blintz is golden brown, gently nudging the side of the blintz with a cake turner and shaking the skillet to loosen the bottom as the blintz cooks. Invert onto a plate. Repeat the process with the remaining batter, stacking the blintzes on the plate as each is cooked.

🖎 For the filling, combine the cottage cheese, sugar and orange peel in a food processor container or blender container. Process until smooth.

🖎 Mound 2 tablespoons of the filling in the center of each blintz. Roll up, tucking in the ends. Arrange the blintzes in a 9x13-inch baking dish.

🖎 Bake at 300 degrees for 15 to 20 minutes or until heated through.

🖎 Serve with your favorite fruit topping or pie filling.

# POTATO MARZIPAN

*Yield: 1 pound*

*2 cups confectioners' sugar*
*¹/₄ cup cold mashed cooked potato*
*8 ounces blanched almonds,*
*   finely ground*
*1 egg white*
*1 tablespoon lemon juice*
*¹/₂ teaspoon almond extract*
*Food coloring (optional)*

☞ Blend the confectioners' sugar and potato in a bowl. Add the almonds.

☞ Blend in the egg white, lemon juice and flavoring.

☞ Knead well by hand or in a food processor.

☞ If desired, divide the dough into small batches. Mix each batch with food coloring.

☞ Shape into flowers, animals, fruit or other figures. Paint the figures with food coloring diluted with water.

**P**OTATO FUDGE

*Yield: 1¹/₄ pounds*

2 ounces unsweetened chocolate
3 tablespoons butter
¹/₃ cup mashed cooked potato
¹/₈ teaspoon salt
1 teaspoon vanilla extract
1 (16-ounce) package
  confectioners' sugar

🌿 Melt the chocolate and butter in a double boiler over hot water. Add the potato, salt and vanilla and mix gently.
🌿 Blend in the confectioners' sugar. Knead or mix until smooth.
🌿 Press into a buttered 8-inch pan. Let cool.
🌿 Cut into squares and remove from the pan.

**P**OTATO CANDY

*Yield: 2¹/₂ pounds*

³/₄ cup diced potato
4 cups confectioners' sugar
4 cups shredded sweetened coconut,
  chopped
1¹/₂ teaspoons vanilla extract
¹/₂ teaspoon salt
4 ounces unsweetened chocolate
  (see Note)

🌿 Boil the potato in water to cover in a saucepan until tender; drain. Mash well and let cool.
🌿 Mix the potato with the confectioners' sugar in a bowl. Stir in the coconut, vanilla and salt and mix well.
🌿 Press into a 9x13-inch pan.
🌿 Melt the chocolate in a double boiler over hot water. Pour over the candy.
🌿 Let cool and cut into squares.

🌿

*Note: Do not allow the water in the double boiler to boil. Chocolate that gets too hot may be streaky when it hardens.*

🌿

# Potato POTPOURRI

## The Wheelbarrow Woman
### *1887?-1945*

Call me Rosalure. My real name's Clydeus
Roxanne. Dunbar. Hells Canyon locals used to
call me Roxie. Dunbarrow Annie. Crazy.
I never had much truck with townsfolk.

there at any rate. I came in when the west
was claimless—sky cornflower blue, blown soil
a ruckus of stern growth. Went first to Thorn
Flat, round the third bend just past Home-

stead, Oregon, where the town's nonesuch
postmistress, Adelaide Georgianna Baker,
passed me a canteen of water and a wood
wheelbarrow rooted to an iron tire. I

thanked her for the questions—where I hailed
from, when I left, with whom, how, why—which
she didn't ask. Don't. I'll give you this:
I followed the folds of hard light

on the mountains, clung to the skirts
of the Snake; forded the Irondyke Ballard
and breakneck steep McGraw creeks. Lava heights
swarmed. Weeks passed. What happened's thus:

The twisted hemp I'd trusted to consign
me to the bench above old Fisher Bar
gave in. I faced the right-about, pulled
back toward Leep Creek. Here I took up

looking after Tom Van Cleave's timeworn
two-room farm, tending hens and a hay
barn. Mostly what I did's make do,
gardening under the grade of a felt

hat, smoking roll-your-owns, packing the
root cellar with potatoes, haying Van Cleave's
fields, hauling both in the loaned brown
barrow as per usual, and splitting cords

of bull pine with umpteen kinds of half-
assed axes. Doing this, I'd see fit to
cloak the full length of my height (6'2")
don my chestnut button shoes, greying

jeans, feather-hemmed gunny sack coat,
and finally the starched white cloth
folded to fit taut like a nun's
coif to keep the sun from singeing

my long bangs. Must be the neighbors
rigged the bridge across the creek, like
they were hellbound to try and help me out.
But when I'd make the trek to Homestead

once a week, I'd lug my hipboots past
midstream so I could cross the surgy
thing myself. Believe you me, I'm unbeholden
to all persons I've dismayed. Plus I kept

smudgeless hundred-dollar bills rolled
like green cigars below a heap of burst
shoes. Might say I made my stray ends meet.
In a bun. I'd smooth it with spit.

In all, the kith of faithful pets—
my chicken Black Boy, retriever Towsy,
countless rattlers and nine highest possible
spirited palominos—mixed the keenest tonic

for what often was just woeful calm,
living in that place alone. Keep in mind:
Nonvenomous stealth and self-dependence
get townspeople talking every time.

Which—now that I'm gone—downright
gets me. Which leaned into and listened
in on finally walked straight out and got me.
To reconcoct me. Let's let that be enough.
— *by Diane J. Raptosh*

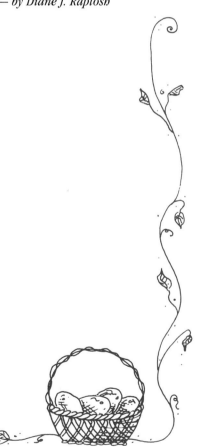

## MR. POTATO HEAD

Mr. Potato Head quickly became one of the country's most popular toys and is still an all-time favorite, with millions sold. Now, if only Barbie would just ditch Ken for Mr. Potato Head . . .

## POTATO STAMPING

*1 potato, 3 to 4 inches in diameter*
*Cookie cutter*
*Sharp paring knife*
*Washable liquid paint*
*Shallow dish*
*Poster paper or brown*
   *wrapping paper*

🖋 Cut the potato into halves crosswise. Draw or stencil a simple design such as a star, heart or letter of the alphabet on the cut side of one half; use a cookie cutter as a pattern if desired. Cut away the background of the design carefully to a depth of $\frac{1}{4}$ inch with a sharp paring knife, leaving a raised design.

🖋 Pour liquid paint into a shallow dish. Dip the raised design into the paint. Stamp onto the paper, repeating the design as desired.

🖋 Use as gift wrap, for book covers or to decorate tissue boxes.

## THE POTATO THAT GREW HAIR

*1 large potato*
*Sharp paring knife*
*2 cotton balls, moistened*
*2 whole cloves*
*1 small carrot or carrot stick*
*Small dish*
*$\frac{1}{2}$ cup water*
*1 tablespoon grass seeds or*
   *bird seeds*

🖋 Cut a $\frac{3}{4}$-inch slice from each end of the potato with a sharp paring knife. Scoop out about 2 tablespoons of the pulp from 1 end. Stuff the cotton balls into the scooped-out area.

🖋 Stick the cloves into the potato to form the eyes. Stick the carrot in to form the nose.

🖋 Place the potato with the straight cut side down in a small dish and add the water. Sprinkle the seeds onto the cotton. Place near a natural light source. Replace the water daily as needed.

🖋 Watch the potato grow "hair" (grass)!

## ACKYARD POTATO GARDEN

*1 garden plot, 3 feet in diameter*
*Shovel and hoe*
*1 potato seedling*
*1 tire*
*Water*
*Fertilizer*

 Work the soil with a shovel and hoe until it is clump-free. Plant the potato seedling 3 to 4 inches deep in the soil. Place the tire around the planting.

 Water and fertilize the plant during the growing season. Mound the soil on top of the potatoes as they grow and poke through the soil, taking care not to cover the leaves.

 When the potatoes are the desired size, harvest the crop and enjoy!

 This is a good gardening activity for children, who can enjoy having a potato-tire garden to call their own.

*Note: It is important to keep the potatoes well covered with soil, as too much light makes them green and bitter. Get Mom or Dad to help fertilize, and follow the manufacturer's directions.*

## NE POTATO-TWO POTATO

One potato, two potato
Three potato, four
Five potato, six potato
Seven potato, more!

 The players stand in a tight circle with arms extended into the center, fists clenched and thumbs on top. One player stands in the center.

 The center player recites the rhyme, lightly tapping each fist in succession. The player whose fist is tapped on the word "more" must put that hand behind his or her back.

 The rhyme is repeated in the same manner until only one fist remains and that player is the winner. The winner is next to recite the rhyme and tap the fists.

## POTATO FLOWER HOLDER

For a potato flower holder, pierce half of a potato with an ice pick in several places. Place the cut side down in a vase of water, then insert flower stems into the holes.

## *I*-D-A-H-O
### JUMP ROPE OR TRAMPOLINE RHYME

I-d-a-h-o
This is where potatoes grow:
    Couer d'Alene, Mountain Home,
Rexburg, Boise, and Shoshone.
    Orofino, Picabo, Pocatello,
Paul, Sun Valley, Caldwell,
    and American Falls.
Nowhere else I'd rather be.
    Idaho's the place for me.

✎ Use the rhyme to set the rhythm for jumping rope or jumping on a trampoline.

## *R*OLL-THE-
### POTATO RELAY

*Chalk or 5-inch paper circle*
*An even number of players*
*2 wooden spoons or sticks*
*2 potatoes*

✎ Draw a 5-inch circle on the sidewalk or driveway with the chalk or tape a 5-inch circle of paper to the floor to play indoors. Draw 2 starting lines 8 feet from the circle on opposite sides of the circle.

✎ Divide the players into 2 equal teams. Arrange each team behind 1 of the starting lines and give the first player in each line a wooden spoon or stick. Place a potato on each line.

✎ At the "go" signal, the first player on each team rolls the potato to the circle and then back to the starting line. The next player then takes the wooden spoon and rolls the potato to the circle in the same manner. The first team to finish wins the game.

# POTATO SACK RACE

*1 wooden stick*
*Several racers*
*1 burlap potato sack for each racer*

☞ Draw a starting line and a turning line for the race in the dirt with the stick. Line the racers up behind the starting line.

☞ Give each racer a burlap potato sack and instruct them to step into the sack and hold the top securely.

☞ At the "go" signal, the racers hop from the starting line to the turning line and back to the starting line. The first player to arrive back at the starting line wins the race.

# BASKET-O-POTATOES

*Wooden stick*
*An even number of players*
*4 potatoes for each player*
*1 basket for each player*

☞ Draw a starting line in the dirt with the stick. Draw 4 circles in front of each player, about 10 feet from the player and about 2 feet apart.

☞ Place 1 potato in the center of each circle. Place 1 basket just behind each starting line.

☞ Line the players up behind the starting line. At the "go" signal each player runs to the first circle, picks up the potato, returns to the starting line and places the potato in the basket; the player then repeats the process to pick up all 4 of the potatoes.

☞ The first player to pick up all 4 of the potatoes in the circle and deposit them in the basket wins the game.

## TIDBITS

Marie Antoinette is

said to have worn

potato flowers in her

hair because the potato

was revered in

France at the time.

## POTATO TRIVIA

"Hot potato" is a term used to describe a particularly difficult or sensitive problem.

 OTATO TAG

*1 wooden stick*
*9 large potatoes, or any odd number of potatoes*
*An even number of players, at least 8*

☞ Draw 2 lines about 10 to 15 feet apart in the dirt with the stick. Draw a circle in the center between the two lines. Place a potato in the circle.

☞ Divide the players into 2 equal teams. Line each team up behind 1 of the lines. Number each player in the lines, starting at opposite ends of the lines, so that the first number on 1 team will face the last number on the opposite team.

☞ A caller calls out a number and the player with that number on each team runs to the center and tries to grab the potato and return to his or her line without being tagged by the other player.

☞ The player who succeeds in taking the potato keeps that potato for his or her team until the end of the game. The game is over when all the potatoes have been used; the team with the most potatoes wins.

 OT POTATO

*4 or more players*
*1 potato*
*Music*

☞ Arrange the players in a circle and give 1 player the potato. Play the music while the players pass the potato clockwise from player to player.

☞ When the music is stopped, the player who is holding the potato is eliminated. Continue playing and stopping the music until only one player is left in the game. The player who is last to be eliminated wins the game.

## igzag Potato

*An equal number of players,*
*at least 8*
*2 potatoes*

☞ Divide the players into 2 teams, with an equal number of players on each team. Line up the players on each team in a row, all facing the same direction.

☞ Give the first player in each row a potato. At the "go" signal the first player passes the potato over his or her head to the person behind. That player must pass it between his or her legs to the person behind. Repeat the over-the-head, between-the-legs passing procedure. The last player runs to the head of the line and repeats the process.

☞ The game continues until the first player is back at the head of the line. The team that accomplishes this first wins the game.

## otato Spoon Race

*An equal number of players,*
*at least 8*
*1 wooden stick*
*2 baskets*
*2 potatoes*
*2 teaspoons*

☞ Divide the players into 2 teams, with an equal number of players on each team. Draw a starting line in the dirt with the stick and arrange the players into 2 rows behind the line.

☞ Place 1 basket in front of each team, 8 feet from the starting line. Place 1 potato on the ground in front of each team. Give the first player in each row a teaspoon.

☞ At the "go" signal, the first player in each row must pick up the potato with the teaspoon, using only 1 hand, run with it to the basket, run back to the team and give the spoon to the next player, going to the back of the line. The next player must run to the basket and retrieve the potato, using the spoon and 1 hand, and return it to the team, placing it on the ground.

☞ The play proceeds until all players have relayed the potato. The first team to do so wins the game.

### Buying and Storing Potatoes

Real Idaho potatoes feature the "Grown in Idaho" seal and have a rounded, elongated shape and a few shallow, deep-brown eyes. Select firm unblemished potatoes. Cut off green spots before cooking to avoid a bitter taste. Damp potatoes decay faster, so store them unwashed. Store away from strong light and heat.

## STEAMING POTATOES

Bring about 1 inch of water to boil in a large saucepan. Place a rack in the saucepan and arrange the potatoes on the rack. Steam, covered, for 15 to 20 minutes or until the potatoes are tender.

## THE POTATO
by Thomas Moore

I'm a careless potato, and care
    not a pin
How into existence I came;
If they planted me drill-wise, or
    dribbled me in,
To me 'tis exactly the same.
The bean and the pea may more
    loftily tower,
But I care not a button for them;
Defiance I nod with my beautiful
    flower
When the earth is hoed up to
    my stem

## POTATO SONG
Sung to the tune of "Peanut, Peanut Butter and Jelly"

Verse 1:
    First you take a shovel and ya
    dig 'em
    Ya dig 'em, ya dig 'em, dig 'em,
    dig 'em.
Chorus:
    Potato, baked potato (pause)
    and butter
    Potato, baked potato (pause)
    and butter.
Verse 2:
    Put them in the oven and ya
    bake 'em
    Ya bake 'em, ya bake 'em,
    bake 'em, bake 'em
Chorus:
Verse 3:
    Cut it with a knife and ya
    butter 'em
    Ya eat 'em, ya eat 'em, eat 'em,
    eat 'em
Chorus: (sing as if your mouth
    is full)

# DOG BISCUITS

This doggie treat is made in the microwave.

*Yield: 18 biscuits or 60 nuggets*

*$^1/_2$ cup all-purpose flour*
*$^3/_4$ cup whole wheat flour*
*$^3/_4$ cup dry skim milk*
*$^3/_4$ cup instant potato flakes*
*$^1/_3$ cup quick-cooking oats*
*2 tablespoons wheat germ*
*$^1/_3$ cup vegetable oil*
*1 egg, beaten*
*$^1/_2$ cup milk*
*2 beef or chicken bouillon cubes*
*1 tablespoon hot water*
*Food coloring (optional)*

🐾 Combine the flours, milk powder, potato flakes, oats, wheat germ, oil, egg and milk in a food processor container or mixer bowl.

🐾 Dissolve the bouillon cubes in the hot water. Add to the flour mixture. Add food coloring if desired. Process until smooth. Shape into a ball and knead on a lightly floured surface for 1 minute.

🐾 Roll $^1/_2$ inch thick and cut with a biscuit or cookie cutter. Arrange 6 biscuits at a time on a 9- or 10-inch microwave-safe plate.

🐾 Microwave at Medium for 6 to 9 minutes or until firm. Remove to a wire rack to cool. Repeat with the remaining biscuits. Store in an airtight container.

🐾

*Give these as Christmas gifts to your furry friends. They will love them!*

🐾

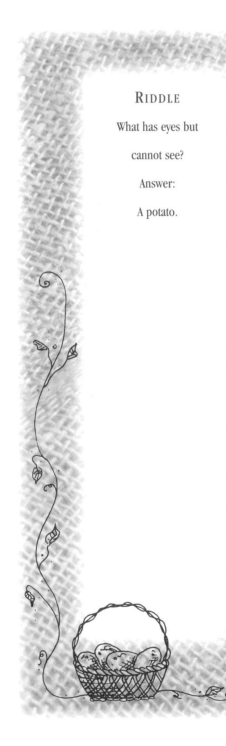

RIDDLE

What has eyes but

cannot see?

Answer:

A potato.

# DOGGIE BIRTHDAY CAKE

This is a treat for your best friends.

2 pounds ground turkey
1½ cups cooked brown rice (½ cup uncooked rice)
½ cup finely chopped carrot
½ cup finely chopped celery
½ cup minced fresh parsley
1 egg, beaten
4 teaspoons minced garlic
1 tablespoon olive oil
2 cups mashed cooked potatoes, divided
Milk
Beet juice

## Garnish
Carrot rounds or shredded carrots

🐾 Combine the turkey, rice, carrot, celery and parsley in a large bowl and mix well. Mix the egg, garlic and oil in a small bowl. Add to the turkey mixture and mix well.

🐾 Pat the mixture into a greased 9x9-inch baking dish. Bake at 350 degrees for 1½ hours or until the turkey is cooked through.

🐾 Let stand until cool. Chill in the refrigerator. Invert onto a serving plate.

🐾 Reserve ½ cup of the mashed potatoes. Spread the remaining mashed potatoes over the top and sides of the "cake."

🐾 Thin the reserved potatoes with enough milk to make of a consistency to pipe through a pastry bag. Add beet juice to produce the desired color. Spoon into a pastry bag fitted with a round or star tip. Pipe the dog's name or other message on the top of the "cake." Add rosettes and garnish with carrot rounds or shredded carrots or other preferred dog treats.

🐾

Don't forget the candles!

🐾

# RESOURCE LIST

These groups provided information or assistance for this cookbook and we wish to
thank them and acknowledge their contribution.  If you want more information
about Idaho or potatoes, please contact them directly.

Boise Convention & Visitors Bureau
Post Office Box 2106
168 North 9th, Suite 200
Boise, Idaho  83701
1-800-635-5240
208-334-7777

Boise Public Library
715 S. Capital
Boise, Idaho  83706
208-384-4076

Coeur d'Alene Area Chamber of
   Commerce
1621 North Third, Suite 100
Post Office Box 850
Coeur D'Alene, Idaho  83814
208-664-3194

James W. Davis, Author
"Aristocrat in Burlap"
Published by the Idaho Potato
   Commission, 1992

Idaho Department of Commerce &
   Tourism
700 West State Street
Post Office Box 83720
Boise, Idaho  83720-0093
208-334-2470

Idaho State Historical Society
Library and Archives
415 North 4th Street
Boise, Idaho  83702
208-334-3356

Idaho Potato Commission
599 West Bannock
Boise, Idaho  83702
208-334-2350

Idaho Potato Expo
Post Office Box 366
Blackfoot, Idaho  83221
208-785-2517

Idaho Grower Shipper's Association
Post Office Box 51100
Idaho Falls, Idaho  83405
208-529-4400

McCall Chamber of Commerce
Post Office Box D
1001 State Street
McCall, Idaho  83638
208-634-7631

Sun Valley/Ketchum Chamber of
   Commerce
Post Office Box 2420
Sun Valley, Idaho  83353
1-800-634-33347
208-726-3423

# $\mathcal{B}$IOGRAPHICAL SKETCHES

🖋 Elaine Ambrose, a Phi Beta Kappa graduate of the University of Idaho, was the first female television news reporter in southern Idaho. Her first novel, *Waiting for the Harvest,* describes a young girl's adventures on a southern Idaho potato farm. A popular motivational speaker and community volunteer, Elaine lives in Boise with her two children.

🖋 Barclay Day is a designer with Graphic Resource, Inc., in downtown Boise. She enjoys creating fun, fresh designs that catch people's eyes and generate interest. She also loves camping, hiking, rollerblading, and playing with her Golden Retriever puppy in the outdoors of Idaho.

🖋 Arthur A. Hart, Director Emeritus of the Idaho Historical Society and author of numerous books and articles on Idaho history and culture, knows from potatoes! As a boy on family farms in Oregon and Washington, he planted potatoes and cultivated and harvested them, with the help of an old horse named Dollie.

🖋 Margaret Hepworth has provided the Junior League of Boise with a variety of volunteer art work since 1989. With a background in drawing and water-color painting, she enjoys doing both commercial and volunteer art projects for the community. Her favorite area of work is children's book illustration.

🖋 Romaine Galey Hon's activities as a volunteer in the Boise Junior League paid off. She got a job she loves—

writing about food for the *Idaho Statesman* newspaper. Before that she was a full-time volunteer and used her journalism training to write about civic projects. The newspaper noticed, and she's still working for it and for the Junior League.

🖋 Broadcast journalist Jyl Hoyt has worked in public radio more than fifteen years. She is Special Projects Unit Director at BSU Radio, based at Boise State University. Jyl's news stories and features are frequently heard on National Public Radio. A former Peace Corps volunteer in Guatemala and Liberia, she also has served as a Fulbright Fellow in Peru.

🖋 Marie Johnson, a native Idahoan, spent her childhood on a farm. When she's not driving her children from one activity to another, she spends her time cooking, quilting, or volunteering in the community. Besides her animated storytelling, she knows a good potato when she sees one.

🖋 Derrick O'Neill is a local storyteller, barrister, and bard. Prone to moments of excess exaggeration, he is quick to point out that his mom is a wonderful person with whom he still spends countless hours. He is a contributing writer and associate editor of the *Eberle Berlin Quarterly*, a legal publication for their clients.

🖋 Raised in Idaho, Diane Raptosh received her M.F.A. from the University of Michigan in 1986. She returned to Idaho in 1990 to teach at Albertson

College of Idaho, where she currently chairs the English Department. Her first book of poetry, *Just West of Now*, was published in 1992 by Guernica Editions. Her second poetry collection, *Labor Songs*, was published by Guernica in the spring of 1997.

🖋 Rebecca Robison has worked in the Boise area as a food and prop stylist since 1988. She has studied with the professional chefs and food stylists at The Culinary Arts and Services in Chicago and with Tante Marie's Cooking School in San Francisco.

🖋 Stan Sinclair is the owner of Sinclair Studio, Inc., a Boise-based advertising photography company. Stan studied photography through the West Coast School of Professional Photography, where he received his Master of Photography degree. Specializing in food, tabletop, people, and photo-illustration photography for the advertising community at large, Stan is known for his creative lighting capabilities and design techniques. Stan's photographs are featured in many books and advertisements and have won many top awards.

🖋 Tim Woodward has enjoyed a long and distinguished career as a columnist and writer for the *Idaho Statesman* newspaper. A native of Boise, he graduated from the University of Idaho. In his free time, he has written five books and plays in a local rock band. He is married with three children.

# CREDITS AND ACKNOWLEDGEMENTS

*Beyond Burlap* was completed because of the dedication and shared vision of countless individuals.
Our deepest gratitude goes to all those listed here and to anyone we may have inadvertently failed to mention.
We thank you for your generous contributions of time, talent, energy, and resources.
The Junior League of Boise is grateful to the following, who joined with us to promote the success
of *Beyond Burlap* and to further our good works in the community:

*Corporations*
ACURA of Boise
Albertson's, Inc.
J.R. Simplot Company
Ore-Ida Foods, Inc.

*Chefs and Culinarians*
Lou Aaron
Marie Galyean
Helcia Graf
Tim Holley
Karen Mangum
John Mortimer
Peter Schott
John Shields
Fred Webster

*Professional Credits*
Barclay Day
Margaret Hepworth
Romaine Galey Hon
Rebecca Robison
Stan Sinclair

*Author Credits*
Kathleen Marion Carr
Arthur A. Hart
Jyl Hoyt
Marie Johnson
Derrick O'Neill
Diane Raptosh
Tim Woodward

# CONTRIBUTORS AND TESTERS

Lou Aaron
Colleen Abel
Lynette Adams
LaFern Ahrens
Lisa Alexander
Candi Allphin
Susan Alt
Heather Amador
Mel Anderson
Julene Andrews
Mede Anton
Susan Applegate
Suzanne Attenborough
Pat Badgley
Jennie Baker
Judy Balcerzak
Judy Balkins
*Barbara Bauer
Carolyn Beaver
Terri Beloit
Helen Bennett
Janet Benoit
Duffy Benton
Brad Bergquist
Renee Bergquist
Marsha Berlin
Lisa Bettis
Sandra Beukelman
Ann Blaschke
*Amy Blickenstaff
Guy Blunham
Sonja Bodine
Anita Bokan
Michelle Bond
Jeannene Boyd
Katrina Bradbury
Laurie Simplot Braun
*Carole Brawley
Marge Briggs
Jeanine Broenheke
Terri Brogan
Edward Brown
Carol Browning

Cheryl Bruehl
Katie Buggmist
Claudia Burgener
Lauri Burgener
Karen Burgess
Carolyn Spicer Burke
Rosa Campbell
Kathleen Marion Carr
Renee Case
Carolyn Casey
Jean Cenarrusa
Dolores Chapman
Joyce Chase
Marlys Churchillo
Jenifer Clawson
Shirlee Coiner
Shar Cox
Elizabeth
        Crandlemire
Beth Creamer
LeAnn Crosby
Wanda Crowley
Courtney Cruce
Barb Curnow
Bill Cutshall
Vicki Cutshall
John Danielson
Maria Davies
Pat Davies
Penelope Davies
Cyndi Davis
Mary Davis
Nancy Davis
Robert DeLong
Rochelle DeLong
Leslie Dietz
Susan DiMotta
Fran Dingel
Deirdre DiOrro
Don Dixon
Mary Donavan
Cheryl Eauclaire
Jan Eby

Jolly Eck
Shelley Eichmann
Rosalie Elam
Joan Elkington
Susie Ellsworth
Shannon Erstad
Lola Evans
Gwen Everman
Evelyn Evert
Valerie Favillo
Sandy Fery
Nancy Fischer
Ada Fish
Sparkle Fisher
Jennifer Fitz
Michael Foley
Becky Fordham
Pam Frei
Lynda Gaber
Marie Galyean
Nancy Gamble
Skip Geroux
Wendy Geyer
Cristine Geyer-Davis
Cathy Giacalone
Leann Gilberg
Robert Ginkel
Tonia Ginkel
Allee Givens
Marcia Glenn
Linda Gossett
Dodie Gray
Ila Greenfield
Robin Greenfield
June Gregg
Bertha Groff
Diane Groff
*Jane Groff
*Kari Guymon
Neccia Hahn
Julianne Haller
Karla Halligan
*Leslie Hampton

Dorothy Hanford
*Polly Hanson
Sharon Hanson
Roxanne Harfmann
Violet Harfmann
Arthur Hart
Barbara Hawley
Beth Hedrick
Shelly Heitzman
Marie Hendrix
Marisa Hendrix
Alice Hennessey
Tom Hennessey
*Margaret Hepworth
Lindy High
Mary Jane Hill
*Rhonda Hill
Denise Hodges
Lynn Hoffmann
Tim Holley
Debra Holmes
Claudia Hon
Romaine Galey Hon
Ed Houdek
Kris House
*Betty Jean Houston
Kelly Houston
Shelly Houston
Margo Huber
Lissa Hummel
Jinks Hunter
Cheryl Hurrle
Karen Hurt
Josh Jackson
Tammy Joerger
*Kathlyn Johans
Donald Johnson
Melanie Johnston
Anna Margaret Jones
Grant Jones
Linda Jones
Rowena Kacewicz
Marcia Karakas

Kelly Kast
Cheri Keith
Celeste Keller
Celia King
Mary Jane King
Nancy Kirk
*Debbie Kling
Kaye Knight
Pat Kohl
Kris Korfanta
Dolores Krause
Shirley Krone
Vicki Kuebler
Jeff Ladwig
Judy Laing
Candy Lambuth
Terri Landa
Kitty Larson
Tracey Latterman
Michelle Leverett
*Suzanne Groff Lierz
Yvonne Lierz
Betty Lisell
Trudy Littman
Patsy Lodge
*Teresa Lyon
*Loretta Madison
Margaret Madison
Amy Maguire
Andy Maier
*Cindy Maier
*Nicole Malmen
Claryce Manweiler
*Diane Manweiler
Kay Manweiler
Carlyn Marion
H. D. Marion
Paula Marshall
Sue Martines
Lee McAllister
Jill McArthur
Mary McCain-Ogle
Michele McCarron

Laurel McClellan
Sue McCutcheon
Josh McKelvey
Kimber McKnight
Jamie McNift
*Nicole Meek
Liz Mello
Zel Mertz
Jan Michaelson
Dake Mickelsen
Heidi Mickelson
Victoria Mickelson
Rene Mifflin
Rhonda Millick
Jane Milza
Liza Morris
Tamara Morrison
Kathy Moyer
Ann Murdoch
Mary Murphey
Peg Murphy
Mary Nahas
Stacie Neely
Avery Tillinghast
    Nelson
Lee Ann Van Vleet
    Nelson
Bibiana Nertney
Jean Norquist
Susan O'Ban
Elizabeth Obbard
Christine Oberholzer
Pat Oberholzer

Chris Ochod
*Patty O'Neill
Judy Osborne
Jeanne Oslund
Chuck Otte
Pat Otte
Dama Overstreet
Mary Owens
Annette Park
Wendy Pennington
Caroline Pereira
Anne Peterson
Bee Pierce
Pat Plumtree
Patty Powell
Kathy Pratt
Linda Prusymskie
Rashelle Quillin
Fran Rabunson
Amy Radue
Michelle Rauer
*Kendis Redding
Debbie Reed
Sue Reents
Kristen Rittenger
Kathy Robert
Marge Roberts
Mary Ann Roberts
Fran Robinson
Hanna Robinson
Amy Roe
Angie Rois
Bob Rois

*Betsy Gaber
    Rosenberg
Leon Rothstein
*Lynn Rubel
Caryn Rutherford
Suzy Ryder
Margarita Santos
Sheila Santos
Lynne Saunders
Christy Saylor
Kathryn Schellenberg
Reci Schmellick
Theresa Schram
Carole Schroeder
Janet Schroeder
Teri Schultz
Terri Schwanz
Sally Scudder
Julie Seiniger
Dennis Shaver
*Kathy Shaver
Ellen Shaw
Sherri Shiefer
Connie Shields
Susanne Shinn
Fae Shouse
Cydney Shubin
Shannon Shumate
Adelia Simplot
*Nora Simpson
Rob Simpson
Virginia Sims
Rena Sinclair

Char Smith
Michel Smith
Susan Smith
Joni Snodgrass
Debra Snow
*LeAnn South
Tom South
Patricia Starkey
Deborah Steinbacher
*Linda Stengle
Edna Stewart
Jeanette Stivens
Mardi Stone
*Martha Strong
Larissa Struwe
Ramona Suarez
*Cindy Sundvik
*Michelle Surkamer
Brenda Tate
Sarah Taylor
Theresa Taylor
Peggy Thiessen
Wayne Thiessen
Barbara Thomas
*Lisa Thomas
Bev Thometz
*Nancy Thompson
Susan Baker Thon
Carol Thornburgh
Elaine Thornburgh
Andrea Thornton-
    Rothstein
Sonia Thyberg

*Kerry Tobin
Bonnie Todeschi
*Cindy Todeschi
Connie Trail
Helen Tropez
Karen Tucker
Terri Turpin
Terri Urbush
Lila Vogele
Sandy von Tagen
Fran Voulelis
Mary Lou Wagner
Shauna Waller
Merle Wells
Mary Wetzler
*Jean Wetzler-Bagley
Oscar Wickersham
Mary Wilcomb
Cherol Williams
*Helen Williams
Jean Wilson
Michele Wilson
*Ronda Wiltse
Carey Wolfe
Graye Wolfe
Timber Wolfe
Chris Wood
Richard Wood
Robin Young
Fred Zerza

* Indicates test team captains

Most heartfelt thanks to our families, who shared the scrubbing, peeling, dicing, mashing,
baking, sautéing, and especially the tasting for *Beyond Burlap*.

# NUTRITION FACTS

Serving Size 1 potato (148g /5.5 oz.)

**Amount Per Serving**

| **Calories** 100 | Calories from Fat 0 |
|---|---|

| | **% Daily Value*** |
|---|---|
| **Total Fat** 0g | 0% |
| Saturated Fat 0g | 0% |
| **Cholesterol** 0mg | 0% |
| **Sodium** 5mg | 0% |
| **Potassium** 720mg | 21% |
| **Total Carbohydrate** 26g | 9% |
| Dietary Fiber 3g | 12% |
| Sugars 3g | |
| **Protein** 4g | |

| | | |
|---|---|---|
| Vitamin A 0% | • | Vitamin C 45% |
| Calcium 2% | • | Iron 6% |
| Thiamin 8% | • | Riboflavin 2% |
| Niacin 8% | • | Vitamin B$_6$ 10% |
| Folate 6% | • | Phosphorous 6% |
| Zinc 2% | • | Magnesium 6% |
| Copper 4% | • | |

*Percent Daily Values are based on a 2,000 calorie diet. Your daily values may be higher or lower depending on your calorie needs:

| | | Calories | 2,000 | 2,500 |
|---|---|---|---|---|
| Total Fat | Less than | | 65g | 80g |
| Sat. Fat | Less than | | 20g | 25g |
| Cholesterol | Less than | | 300mg | 300mg |
| Sodium | Less than | | 2,400mg | 2,400mg |
| Potassium | | | 3,500mg | 3,500mg |
| Total Carbohydrate | | | 300g | 375g |
| Dietary Fiber | | | 25g | 30g |

Calories per gram:
Fat 9 • Carbohydrate 4 • Protein 4

# $\mathcal{N}$O-SALT SEASONING

*Salt is an acquired taste and can be significantly reduced in the diet by learning to use herbs and spices instead. When using fresh herbs, use 3 times the amount of dried herbs. Begin with small amounts to determine your favorite tastes. A dash of fresh lemon or lime juice can also wake up your taste buds.*

## HERB BLENDS TO REPLACE SALT

☛ Combine all the ingredients in a small airtight container. Add several grains of rice to prevent caking.

**No-Salt Surprise Seasoning** — 2 teaspoons garlic powder and 1 teaspoon each of dried basil, oregano and dehydrated lemon juice.

**Pungent Salt Substitute** — 3 teaspoons dried basil, 2 teaspoons each of summer savory, celery seeds, cumin seeds, sage and marjoram, and 1 teaspoon lemon thyme; crush with a mortar and pestle.

**Spicy No-Salt Seasoning** — 1 teaspoon each cloves, pepper and coriander, 2 teaspoons paprika and 1 tablespoon dried rosemary; crush with a mortar and pestle.

## HERB COMPLEMENTS

**Beef** — bay leaf, chives, cumin, garlic, hot pepper, marjoram, rosemary

**Pork** — coriander, cumin, garlic, ginger, hot pepper, savory, thyme

**Poultry** — garlic, oregano, rosemary, savory, sage

**Cheese** — basil, chives, curry, dill, marjoram, oregano, parsley, sage, thyme

**Fish** — chives, coriander, dill, garlic, tarragon, thyme

**Fruit** — cinnamon, coriander, cloves, ginger, mint

**Bread** — caraway, marjoram, oregano, poppy seeds, rosemary, thyme

**Salads** — basil, chives, tarragon, parsley, sorrel

**Vegetables** — basil, chives, dill, tarragon, marjoram, mint, parsley, pepper

## BASIC HERB BUTTER

☛ Combine 1 stick unsalted butter, 1 to 3 tablespoons dried herbs or twice that amount of minced fresh herbs of choice, $\frac{1}{2}$ teaspoon lemon juice and white pepper to taste. Let stand for 1 hour or longer before using.

## BASIC HERB VINEGAR

☛ Heat vinegar of choice in a saucepan; do not boil. Pour into bottle; add 1 or more herbs of choice and seal bottle. Let stand for 2 weeks before using.

# HERBS AND SPICES

*Use fresh whole **herbs** when possible. When fresh herbs are not available, use whole dried herbs that can be crushed just while adding. Store herbs in airtight containers away from the heat of the stove. Fresh herbs may be layered between paper towels and dried in the microwave on HIGH for 2 minutes or until dry. **Spices** should be stored in airtight containers away from the heat of the stove or in the refrigerator. Add ground spices toward the end of the cooking time to retain maximum flavor. Whole spices may be added at the beginning but should also have a small amount of additional spices added near the end of cooking time.*

**Allspice:** Pungent aromatic spice, whole or in powdered form. It is excellent in marinades, particularly in game marinade, or in curries.

**Basil:** Can be chopped and added to cold poultry salads. If the recipe calls for tomatoes or tomato sauce, add a touch of basil to bring out a rich flavor.

**Bay leaf:** The basis of many French seasonings. It is added to soups, stews, marinades and stuffings.

**Celery seeds:** Use whole or ground in salad dressings, sauces, pickles or meat, cheese, egg and fish dishes.

**Chili powder:** Made from dried red chile peppers, this spice ranges from mild to fiery depending on the type of chile pepper used. Used especially in Mexican cooking, it is a delicious addition to eggs, dips and sauces.

**Chives:** Available fresh, dried or frozen, it can be substituted for fresh onion or shallot in nearly any recipe.

**Cinnamon:** Ground from the bark of the cinnamon tree, it is delicious in desserts as well as savory dishes.

**Coriander:** Seeds used whole or ground, this slightly lemony spice adds an unusual flavor to soups, stews, chili dishes, curries and desserts.

**Cumin:** A staple spice in Mexican cooking. Use in meat, rice, cheese, egg and fish dishes.

**Curry powder:** A blend of several spices, this gives Indian cooking its characteristic flavor.

**Garlic:** One of the oldest herbs in the world, it must be carefully handled. For best results, press or crush the garlic clove.

**Ginger:** The whole root used fresh, dried or ground is a sweet, pungent addition to desserts or oriental-style dishes.

**Mint:** Use fresh, dried or ground with vegetables, desserts, fruits, jelly, lamb or tea. Fresh sprigs of mint make attractive aromatic garnishes.

**Mustard (dry):** Ground mustard seeds bring a sharp bite to sauces or may be sprinkled sparingly over poultry or other foods.

**Nutmeg:** Use the whole spice or a bit of freshly ground for flavor in beverages, breads and desserts. A sprinkle on top is both a flavor enhancer and an attractive garnish.

**Oregano:** A staple, savory herb in Italian, Spanish, Greek and Mexican cuisines. It is very good in dishes with a tomato foundation, especially in combination with basil.

**Parsley:** Use this mild herb as fresh sprigs or dried flakes to flavor or garnish almost any dish.

**Pepper:** Black and white pepper from the pepperberry or peppercorn, whether whole, ground or cracked, is the most commonly used spice in or on any food.

**Poppy seeds:** Use these tiny, nutty-flavored seeds in salad dressings, breads, cakes or as a flavorful garnish for cheese, rolls or noodle dishes.

**Rosemary:** This pungent herb is especially good in poultry and fish dishes and in such accompaniments as stuffings.

**Sage:** This herb is a perennial favorite with all kinds of poultry and stuffings.

**Tarragon:** One of the fines herbes. Goes well with all poultry dishes whether hot or cold.

**Thyme:** Usually used in combination with bay leaf in soups, stews and sauces.

**Turmeric:** Ground from a root related to ginger, this is an essential in curry powder. Also used in pickles, relishes, cheese and egg dishes.

# CHEESE CHART

| Cheese | Goes With | Used For | Flavor, Texture |
|---|---|---|---|
| **Bel Paese** (Italy) | Fresh fruit French bread | Dessert Snack | Spongy, mild, creamy yellow interior |
| **Bleu** (France) | Fresh fruit Bland crackers | Dessert Dips, Salads | Marbled, blue-veined, semisoft, piquant |
| **Brie** (France) | Fresh fruit | Dessert Snack | Soft, edible crust, creamy |
| **Brick** (U.S.) | Crackers Bread | Sandwiches Snack | Semisoft, mild, cream-colored to orange |
| **Camembert** (France) | Apples | Dessert Snack | Mild to pungent, edible crust, yellow |
| **Cheddar** (England) | Fresh fruit Crackers | Dessert Cooking, Snack | Mild to sharp, cream-colored to orange |
| **Cottage** (U.S.) | Canned or Fresh fruit | Fruit salads Cooking | Soft, moist, mild, white |
| **Cream** (U.S.) | Crackers and Jelly | Dessert, Cooking Sandwiches | Soft, smooth, mild, white |
| **Edam** (Holland) | Fresh fruit | Dessert Snack | Firm, mild, red wax coating |
| **Feta** (Greece) | Greek salad | Salad Cooking | Salty, crumbly, white |
| **Gorgonzola** (Italy) | Fresh fruit Italian bread | Dessert Snack | Semisoft, blue-veined, piquant |
| **Gouda** (Holland) | Fresh fruit Crackers | Dessert Snack | Softer than Edam, mild, nutty |

| CHEESE | GOES WITH | USED FOR | FLAVOR, TEXTURE |
|--------|-----------|----------|-----------------|
| **Gruyère** (Switzerland) | Fresh fruit | Dessert Fondue | Nutty, bland, firm, tiny holes |
| **Liederkranz** (Germany) | Onion slices Dark bread | Dessert Snack | Edible light orange crust, robust, soft |
| **Limburger** (Belgium) | Dark bread Bland crackers | Dessert | Soft, smooth, white, robust, aromatic |
| **Mozzarella** (Italy) | Italian foods | Cooking Pizza | Semisoft, delicate, mild, white |
| **Muenster** (Germany) | Crackers Bread | Sandwiches Snack | Semisoft, mild to mellow |
| **Parmesan** (Italy) | Italian foods | Cooking | Hard, brittle, sharp, light yellow |
| **Port Salut** (France) | Fresh fruit Crackers | Dessert Snack | Buttery, semisoft |
| **Provolone** (Italy) | Italian foods | Cooking Dessert | Salty, smoky, mild to sharp, hard |
| **Ricotta** (Italy) | Italian foods | Cooking Fillings | Soft, creamy, bland, white |
| **Roquefort** (France) | Bland crackers Fresh fruit | Dips, Salads Dessert | Semisoft, sharp, blue-veined, crumbly |
| **Stilton** (England) | Fresh fruit Bland crackers | Dips, Salads Dessert | Semisoft, sharp, blue-veined |
| **Swiss** (Switzerland) | Fresh fruit French bread | Cooking, Snack Sandwiches | Sweetish, nutty, holes, pale yellow |

# INDEX

# BEYOND BURLAP

### *Idaho's Famous Potato Recipes*

Please send _____ copies of ***Beyond Burlap***  @ $19.95 each  $_____

Shipping @ $3.00 each  $_____

Idaho residents add 5% sales tax (or current tax rate)  $_____

TOTAL  $_____

*Reduced rates available on orders of 6 or more books. Please inquire by phone, fax or mail.*

## SHIP TO:

Name _____

Address _____

City _____ State _____ Zip Code_____

Method of Payment  _____ Check  _____ Credit Card

*Please make checks payable to The Junior League of Boise*

### MAIL ORDER FORM TO:
The Junior League of Boise
Attention: ***Beyond Burlap***
5266 Franklin Road
Boise, Idaho 83705

Visa/MasterCard Number _____

Expiration Date _____

Signature _____

To order by phone and credit card, call toll-free, 1-888-340-5754, or (208) 342-8851 or fax (208) 342-4901.
Please allow 6 weeks for delivery.

*Proceeds from the sale of this book support the good works of the Junior League of Boise, Inc.*